AFTER PRINCIPLES

REVISIONS

A Series of Books on Ethics

General Editors:

Stanley Hauerwas and Alasdair MacIntyre

After Principles

GARRETT BARDEN

University of Notre Dame Press
Notre Dame   London

Copyright © 1990 by
University of Notre Dame Press
Notre Dame, Indiana 46556
All Rights Reserved
Manufactured in the United States of America

Library of Congress Cataloging-in-Publication Data

Barden, Garrett.
    After principles / Garret Barden.
        p.   cm. — (Revisions : v. 9)
    Includes bibliographical references.
    ISBN 0-268-00626-1
    1. Ethics. 2. Conduct of life. 3. Tradition (Philosophy)
I. Title. II. Series.
BJ37.B27   1990
170—dc20   89-40743

Contents

Preface

This essay is addressed to the professional philosopher and to the common reader. It considers a topic familiar to both, namely, that there are, or seem to be, fundamental and irreconcilable differences of opinion about how humans should live. This topic is as old as Western philosophy but has gained new impetus in recent years with the discovery of incommensurable paradigms, mutually incompatible presuppositions, irreconcilable epistemes. It is claimed that there is no set of basic given or innate propositions common to all human beings. A consequence would seem to be that we are confined within horizons from which we cannot escape and which render conversation and agreement, in the final analysis, impossible; that we speak separate languages between which there is no translation.

The thesis propounded here is that there are, indeed, no given or innate propositions; that our traditions do place us in different, and, at least sometimes, mutually incompatible, horizons; but that our traditions, with their irreconcilable basic presuppositions, are themselves not ultimate; that what is ultimate is a set of operations that gives rise to traditions; that this set of ultimate operations is common and that, consequently, we are not irredeemably confined within the limits of our present selves.

We may in practice abandon the attempt to discuss and persuade; we may recognize that it is, on this occasion, either not worth the effort or not likely to be successful. But, when faced with another human being, we never accept him or her as, in principle, confined

within some horizon that we cannot share; as, in principle, playing a language game of which we cannot know
the rules, as irremediably bounded by paradigms or
presuppositions other than our own. Neither do we
experience ourselves as, in the end, intellectually committed to a set of invulnerable propositions, for which
we are not responsible, and from which we may confidently deduce our world.

But if we hold that conversation is possible, we know,
too, that it is difficult. We discover ourselves within our
traditions without which every aspect of human living
would regularly revert to chaos. It is these that we must
first understand if we are to discover where and what
our bases, as a matter of fact, are. And yet, as we learn
from tradition, we learn that tradition is the discovery
of earlier generations and so fundamentally open to
question. Thus, we become responsible for our tradition:
not that it is, but that it survives. Our tradition is where
we are fated to begin. Where we end is our responsibility,
even if we exercise that responsibility in a world in part
decided by others, in part the unintended consequences
of intended action, in part the product of the play of
nature, in part our unknown selves, and entirely, or not
at all, providential.

We are educated by and within our several traditions
that suggest to us our vulnerable criteria, and in that
educational process we discover our own responsibility.
Our ethical action is properly understood, not as an
ethic of duty and obedience but, more deeply, as an
ethic of responsible invention and creativity.

Writing, too, is an ethical activity. It has its own
specific character but it shares with all ethical activity
the attempt to create, from within the tradition and
within the particular situation in which the writer finds
him or herself, a future for which the author takes
responsibility. The writer's tradition is never simply earlier writing, and concentration on this may mislead.

Nevertheless, earlier writing has usually played a large part that it is good to acknowledge. The following are some of those writers or writings that seem to me to have been most significant in the formation of the tradition from which this work begins: Plato, *Gorgias*, *Statesman*; Aristotle, *Nicomachean Ethics*; Aquinas, *Summa Theologiae*, *Commentary on Aristotle's Ethics*; Hobbes, *Leviathan*, *Dialogue Between a Philosopher and a Student of the Common Laws of England*; Spinoza, *Ethica more geometrica demonstrata*; Kant, *Groundwork for a Metaphysic of Morals*; Hegel, *Philosophy of Right*; Sartre, *Being and Nothingness*, *Les carnets de la drôle de guerre*; Collingwood, *An Essay on Metaphysics*; Kelsen, *Pure Theory of Law*; Lonergan, *Insight*, *The Concept of Verbum in the Writings of Thomas Aquinas*, and other writings; Villey, *Seize leçons de philosophie du droit*; MacIntyre, *After Virtue*. Some others are mentioned in the Notes, which I have kept to a minimum and which serve as well to indicate further questions.

Our background is dialectically composed of writings with which we disagree as much as of those with which we are in accord—this dialectical character of tradition is not peculiar to writers—and we are often as much in debt to those whom we consider opponents as to those with whom we agree. There is a passage near the beginning of Hobbes's *Dialogue Between a Philosopher and a Student of the Common Laws of England* where the student claims that laws should be founded on reason and the philosopher poses the simple question, Whose reason? As a matter of autobiographical fact, Hobbes's question and his answer were the beginning of this essay.

Indebtedness is almost endless: to colleagues, students, friends, family. To opponents. Even to enemies whom, in the Christian tradition, we are enjoined to love, and must, therefore, be presumed to have. We are dialectically indebted to our entire past—what we reject as well

as what we accept; what has warped us as much as
what has contributed to our well-being. The responsible
creation of the present is our only possibility of
repayment.

Garrett Barden
Cork

11 August 1989

1. Moral action without theory

No human community fails to distinguish between good and bad actions. No normal person reaches adulthood without learning what is thought good and what bad in the community. As humans are naturally linguistic beings but realize their natural linguistic capacity in the language of their community, so, too, are they naturally ethical or moral but realize this ethical capacity within the ethics of their community.[1]

This distinction between good and bad actions is not theoretical; there may well be little or no discussion of the meaning of *good* and *bad* or of the various other discriminatory words in common use. But the communal culture presents some actions as good, some as bad, some as honorable, some as mean, some as generous, some as miserly, some as magnanimous, some as petty, some as brave, some as cowardly, and so on, through the culturally available categories of praise and blame.

The passage from birth to adulthood is through an intellectual and sensitive learning of that cultural discrimination that is, to a large extent, the core of the culture itself. This elaborate and subtle discrimination of actions is the culture's complex definition of what it means to be fully human. This cultural definition is not theoretic and, often, is not associated with any theoretical or even immediately pretheoretical discussion. It has to do with an operative understanding, present in every human society, that humanity is not simply a given fact but an achievement. Rites of passage through

1

which a young person goes on the way to adulthood
are more or less obscure symbols of this understanding.[2]

Socrates thought that his questioning of the young
men of Athens showed that they did not know the
meaning of their everyday discriminatory words, that
they did not know what justice meant and what bravery.
But, of course, in the practice of everyday speech, they
knew very well what they meant. They knew that Leonidas, who held the pass at Thermopylae, was brave.
They knew, in a very general way, that bravery was
that kind of thing. They rarely made mistakes in their
use of the word though they might at times dispute
whether such and such an action or proposal was brave
or simply foolhardy. They were satisfied, as Socrates was
not, with such pragmatic common sense. But they had
no theory of bravery and theory was Socrates' goal.[3]

The Athenians had no theory of bravery, nor of
magnanimity, nor of justice, nor of prudence, but their
songs, stories, plays, and laws were expressions of their
common knowledge and appreciation of these virtues.
They knew that Leonidas was brave and that to be
brave was valuable.

When the child learns how the culture discriminates
actions, what is learned is not simply sociologically or
ethnologically interesting fact; what is learned are values.
The child learns what bravery is by learning to admire
Leonidas and other exemplars. Such learning is gradual
and occurs in countless different ways. Hearing the story
of Leonidas is only one. The ethics of a community
may be expressed in stories, laws, and proverbs but is
also, and primarily, expressed in everyday actions and
in responses to actions. The child learns how to admire
by living intelligently and sensitively with those who
admire things and learns what is admirable by learning
what, in everyday practice, is admired.

Stories, songs, laws, and proverbs commonly express
and concentrate upon what seem the more important

features of the communal ethics. The fact that the story of Leonidas persists shows not only what bravery is, not only that it is admirable, but that it is important. Often the stories told of the recurrent problems of living and that bravery was important, at least in part, because bravery was often needed. The singular event—Leonidas' holding Thermopylae—becomes typical in story; while remaining full of circumstantial details—some of these, perhaps, historically true, others invented to serve the purpose of the narrative—the recounted event becomes a type for similar events. The narrative enables the listeners to classify events and, at the same time, to evaluate them. Narrative is a subtle evaluative classification and thus becomes a major carrier of a community's ethic. The narrative is distinct from the action it purports to describe in that the details, whether real or invented, are chosen to highlight the meaning; narrative is a complex image in which the listener or reader discerns value.

I have taken the story of Leonidas as an example of the way in which a culture may present its discriminations. The rhetoric of the story is not the imperative rhetoric of the command but a more ambiguous rhetoric of presentation. The story would be almost unintelligible if the hearers did not grasp that Leonidas' action was admirable. The epitaph to Leonidas and his companions

> Go, tell the Spartans, you who pass by,
> That here, obedient to their laws, we lie

would have a very different place in Western civilization had the general response to it been disdain or repudiation. For better or worse, Western civilization has been what it has been, in part, because Leonidas' action has been thought admirable.[4]

The rhetoric of the Decalogue or Ten Commandments is, obviously, a rhetoric of command. Its place in Western culture has given pride of place to the rhetoric of command as the prime carrier—to the almost total imaginative and theoretic exclusion of other carriers—of the communal ethic. We are, I think, inclined to think of an ethic as a code presented as the Decalogue is. I have stressed the presentational rhetoric of the story in an effort to show that the communal ethic appears in many ways and covers all aspects of ordinary human living.

Because the Decalogue appears in codified form it looks more like theory than does a story but it is not. It is simply another rhetorical expression of the ethic of a people. It deals with the relation between the people of Israel and Yahweh, their god, and with their relations with one another. The activities written of in the Decalogue are written of again and again in different rhetorical forms throughout the Old Testament and, indeed, the Decalogue itself, which became detached from its context within later Christian culture, occurs within the larger framework of the dominant rhetorical form of the Old Testament, which is that of the dialogue between Yahweh and his people.[5]

To suggest that moral or ethical action within a culture occurs without theory is not to suggest that there is no thought, no reflection, but simply automatic responses. Communities differ from one another not only in the spare content of their ethic at any given time but in the manner in which they reflect upon this traditional content. So, among the Hebrews, there was a continual prayerful reflection on the tradition within the dominant rhetorical form of the dialogue as well as the more analytic Talmudic tradition, which, of course, also is clearly rooted in the Pentateuch. These traditions need not be opposed, although they may be, and, within the rhetoric of the New Testament, to some extent are. Within the tradition of prayerful reflection, the tradition of the prophets, there are development and simplification so that Christ's summation of the law and the prophets into the two great commandments of loving God and one's neighbor is not out of keeping with what had been happening, as is plain in this passage from the prophet Micah (6:6–8):

> With what gift shall I come into the presence of Yahweh? Must I give my first born for what I have done wrong, the fruit of my body for my own sin? What is good has been explained to you, man: this is what Yahweh asks of you, only this: to act justly, to love tenderly and to walk humbly with your God.

Here again is the fundamental dialogic form as well as the rhetoric of commandment. But there is not here ethical theory. There is, quite simply, one expression of an ethic.

Questions as to whether what is commanded is good, precisely because it is commanded, or commanded because it is good, simply do not arise within the prophetic horizon. Neither is the question of one's own responsibility for action properly asked. The human person is dramatically represented as responsible, and one of the functions of Yahweh in the narrative is to show the significance of that responsibility. Nowhere in the Old Testament is a character clearly taken over by Yahweh as characters are taken over by the gods in early Greek myths. There is a passage in 1 Samuel (19:6) where an "evil spirit of Yahweh enters Saul," who then tries to kill David, and there are stories of possession in the New Testament, but, in general, the dramatic place of Yahweh in the Old Testament is very unlike the place of the gods in the Greek myths. The difference is not the difference between common sense and theory but between two different common senses, two distinct cultures.

Examples may at once illuminate and mislead. Because I have taken examples from the Greeks or the Hebrews the reader may be misled into thinking that I am suggesting that the communication of an ethic is something old, arcane, and classical. This is not so. The television film and the average novel present an ethic just as much as does the *Odyssey* or *Iliad*.

2. The ethical field

Every community presents and develops its ethic in a variety of rhetorical forms and in the practice of everyday life. It can happen that, in the course of a community's ethical reflection, certain rhetorical forms dominate almost to the exclusion of others and begin to define the ethical field. In Western culture, the Decalogue has defined the field in two ways. The first domination has already been mentioned: because the Decalogue is a series of commands, it is often taken for granted that an ethic is properly, even exclusively, defined by commands. The second domination is that the content of the Decalogue may be taken to define the ethical or moral. These two dominations have significantly distorted the development of an adequate ethical theory.

The ethical or moral field may be defined as the domain of deliberation and choice.[6] Ethical action has to do with realizing a possibility over which one has control and for which one is responsible. Perhaps precisely because examples are endless we often take extreme cases—for example, whether or not killing is ever justified—that can inculcate or reinforce the idea that the ethical covers only a narrow band of living. If the ethical is the domain of deliberation and choice, whether or not one should take a second chocolate is an ethical matter, even if often quite trivial. Whether or not one should get married and to this person is an ethical issue. Whether or not one should divorce; whether or not one should accept the offer of a new job; whether or not one should buy a new car or a new shirt; whether or

not one should read this book; whether or not one
should eat meat; whether or not one should use aerosol
sprays; whether or not one should vote for a particular
candidate; whether or not one should give up smoking;
whether or not one should support the plan to build a
chemical factory in one's town; whether or not one
should engage in a war of liberation; whether or not
one should go on a diet; whether or not one should
allow one's children to watch unlimited television—these
are all questions within the ethical field.

I have deliberately mixed what seem to me trivial and
what seem to me important for two reasons. First, the
distinction between the trivial and the important is
insufficiently noticed in ethical theory in general and,
because it is unnoticed, it is often surreptitiously used
to distinguish between the ethical and the nonethical.
Whether or not to take a second chocolate is sometimes
thought not to be an ethical question; it is considered
nonethical, I suggest, because it is considered trivial
although there is rarely any explicit reason given for
excluding it from the ethical domain. Once the distinction has been made explicitly, I think it becomes plain
that the more radical definition of the ethical field as
the domain of deliberation and choice is the more coherent. Within that domain we can make further dis-
tinctions, one of which is between the important and
the trivial. Second, what is important and what trivial
is not simply given and is not necessarily agreed. Nor
is what is trivial for one person necessarily trivial for
another. Indeed, the ethical culture of a community
often changes by changing the relative importance of a
recurrent activity, and communities differ from each
other sometimes because of different degrees of importance they attach to particular actions.

That the ethical domain or field is the domain of
deliberation and choice is a cardinal element in the

theory being put forward here and, for that if for no other reason, it is necessary to insist upon it.

In everyday English and, indeed, in a great deal of philosophical English the adjective *moral* is often used quite differently from the usage adopted in this work in harmony with the theory. The following expressions are typical:

> She acted for moral rather than selfish reasons.
> That was a purely practical rather than a
>   moral reason.
> He did that for immoral reasons.
> He chose that course for nonmoral reasons.

In a fluid, commonsensical, inexact, and, eventually, I think, fundamentally misleading way we understand such expressions well enough for everyday conversation and, although theory, when generally accepted in a culture, tends eventually to influence usage, my main concern is not the reform of speech. But I should like to make it quite clear that this usage is totally inappropriate to the theory I am putting forward and is systematically obfuscating.[7]

In the theory put forward here, "selfish" reasons are "moral" reasons inasmuch as they are reasons for action within the domain of deliberation and choice. I do not at all suggest that reasons for action may not be further characterized as "selfish," "generous," and so on; nor do I suggest that reasons cannot be criticized. In fact, the whole burden of the theory is that criticism is possible. But the adjective *moral* is used to qualify a reason for action within a domain or to qualify an action within that domain.

Suppose, for example, that I have an opportunity to embezzle some funds by falsifying my expenses. The proposed action is within the moral or ethical domain because, clearly, it is a matter of deliberation and choice. I may decide not to falsify my expenses. I may so decide because (1) I think the chances of being discovered are too great and the consequences of discovery too undesirable for me to take the risk or because (2) I think that falsifying my expenses depletes the communal fund unjustly and gives me more than what is due to me. I have no wish to deny that there are crucially important differences between these reasons, but these differences should not be allowed to obscure the crucial analytic fact that both are reasons for action within the moral domain and so both are moral reasons.

As a matter of fact, although I have presented no argument for this view, I think that the first reason is a bad one and the second reason a good one. If any reader agrees with me, then what is shown is that author and reader on this occasion share a common culture. Whether someone who did not already share this common culture could be persuaded to do so is a further question.

It is not difficult to find examples where, I suspect, I may differ from at least some readers in my evaluation of reasons. Suppose that a man and woman sexually attracted but not married to each other had the opportunity of having intercourse. They might decide to forego the pleasure because (1) there was no safe contraceptive method available to them at the time and they did not want to risk pregnancy or because (2) they shared a common culture within which intercourse outside marriage was considered wrong. Again here are two very different reasons, but I see no really coherent reason to dub one practical and the other moral. And, again as a matter of autobiographical fact, I think of the first of these reasons as good although not wholly adequate and the second as critically in need of development and interpretation although historically associated with an important and valuable tradition of reflection of which it is hardly more than the decadent residue.

The habit of withholding the description "moral" from certain kinds of reasons spills over into the habit of withholding the description "moral" from certain actions within the domain of deliberation and choice precisely because these excluded actions do not seem to be ever undertaken for "moral" reasons. So, some readers may have balked at some of the entries in the list of moral actions given previously. In my experience the commonplace examples of moral actions are whether or not one should kill someone, whether or not one should steal, whether or not one should have sexual intercourse. I do not deny that these are examples of moral actions: I have taken them as examples a moment ago. However, the generally restricted range of the examples only reinforces the prejudice that moral actions are a fairly restricted class of actions and that there are many actions within the domain of deliberation and choice that are not moral. Whether or not to get married to this person is not often taken as a paradigm of a moral action, and yet I suspect that it is one of the most important moral decisions taken by many people.

Analytically there are two distinct questions: whether or not to get married; whether or not to get married to this person. Examine for a moment the second. It is within the domain of deliberation and choice; indeed, it is not easy to find a clearer example in our culture of an action so obviously within the domain. Many people deliberate long before making the decision. They consider reasons for and against. They ask whether or not the reasons are sufficient. The example is almost the paradigm of the moral action. Yet it is rarely so considered. Why?

There are, I think, at least two important reasons why the decision to get married is rarely taken as an example of a moral action. They are these. First, there is no law in our culture that can plausibly be invoked enjoining me to marry this person. Behind this reason is the theory that without law there is no morality whether this dictum is understood in the Occamian, Hobbesian, or Kantian sense. Second, it is not common in our culture to think of the decision to marry or the decision not to marry as possibly involving fault or, in an older terminology, sin. Behind this reason is a slightly different acceptance of law, a concentration on the fault or sin involved in breaking the law, and, finally, a concept of fault or sin as breaking a law.

If that analysis is correct, then it appears that the restriction of the moral to a subset of actions within the domain of deliberation and choice rests on an ethical theory that has been surreptitiously introduced. My suggested definition of the moral or ethical domain— which, I suggest, is the definition accepted by Plato, Aristotle, and Aquinas and fairly explicitly rejected by Occam in favor of the modern, narrower, and surreptitiously theoretical definition—states simply that there are activities that are not subject to deliberation and choice and actions that are subject to deliberation and choice. The terms "ethical" and "moral" are names denoting those actions subject to deliberation and choice. The study of ethical action is simply the study of those actions. This is, of course, theoretical but the theory is quite explicit and basic: if there are such actions, then they can be studied and ethical theory is possible; if there are no such actions, then ethical theory is not possible since its field of study does not exist. Whether or not there are such actions is a proper and important question, but it is not the question raised in this monograph, in which the occurrence of actions that are the result of deliberation and choice is presupposed.

3. Ethical theory

Ethical theory is a Greek invention, but there is no reason to suppose that whenever a Greek philosopher discussed ethical issues he was engaged in theory. Much of Plato is, I think, not theory but reflection, and if it is very different from that of the Hebrew prophets, the difference is rhetorical and does not correspond to the distinction between reflection and theory or between philosophy and religion. Plato's dialogues are in the literary form of a court case rather than in the form of a dialogue between Yahweh and his people.

But Plato also engages in theory as the prophets do not. In *Phaedo* he asks of the relation between the concrete just action and justice, a question that simply does not arise within the prophetic horizon. It is a properly theoretical question focusing on the nature of criterion. I want to discuss it briefly because both the question and its answer are, I think, the source of a perennial philosophical difficulty.

But first an ambiguity must be dispatched. Commonly humans try to understand particular situations in the light of general ideas. We experience no difficulty in doing this; often we have no difficulty in discerning that the situation before us is a certain kind of situation or that one case is like another. Whenever a legal system, however simple, develops, its practitioners become adept at comparing cases. But this subtle and intelligent practice is not theory. The shift to theory occurs when the thinker turns from the exercise of this spontaneous and intelligent practice to focus on the practice itself and to raise questions about the relation that grounds the prac-

tice. And this is, of course, what Plato did, for if there
is one characteristic question running through the whole
of Plato, it is the question of the universal and the
particular.[8]

Plato's forms have many functions, one of which is
to serve as criteria in judgment. Thus, in the *Meno* the
slave boy recognizes the solution because he comes upon
the form, the vision of which casts out all doubt. Similarly, in the *Statesman*, the Royal Ruler sees the form
of justice and this illuminates his contact with the
everyday world so that he knows exactly and beyond
question what is just.

In stark contrast with the Royal Ruler, the ordinary
judge must follow the rules established by the Royal
Ruler. Plato does not think that these laws laid will
exactly fit every situation. Indeed, quite explicitly, he
expects that they will not always do so. But even in
these cases, when the ordinary judge knows that the
laws do not fit, he must nonetheless apply them, for he
lacks the vision of the form of justice and so any
deviation by him from the rule would be random and
without criterion, since he would have nothing against
which to compare his judgment.

Plato never thought that a judgment was right simply
because it followed the law—he does not subscribe to
the Occamian idea that where there is no law there is
no injustice[9]—but he does hold that for ordinary judges,
because of their ignorance of the form, the only recourse
is to follow the law. So the law becomes a kind of second
level or transferred criterion. The first and only adequate
criterion of justice is the form and, ideally, the Royal
Ruler would make a judgment in each case. The second,
derived, and inadequate criterion is the law that is
established by the Royal Ruler after his vision of the
form. Still, despite its inadequacy, the law is a criterion
for the ignorant. The patient follows the doctor's advice,
which acts as a criterion, but the dosage is right not

because the doctor advised it, but because it is in fact right and the doctor knew it was right because he had the vision of the form. Thus, in a derived, inadequate, and fallible way, the law reveals the fact.

When Plato is read in this way he comes closer to Aristotle, but a crucial difference between them remains the possibility of prudence. Prudence is proper to the Royal Ruler, who grasps the just in the particular case because he can compare it with the form of justice. This prudential judgment, in Plato's account, is closed to the ordinary judge. In Aristotle's account, on the contrary, prudence is precisely what the ordinary judge needs. But Plato never suggests that something is right because of the law, although he has sometimes been so interpreted and this version of criterion comes down through the Occamian tradition by way of Hobbes, Selden, Austin, and Kelsen, among others.

A further and centrally important feature of the Platonic criterion is that it is conceived as already there, fully formed and perfect. Even the Royal Ruler must refer to the perfect form, which already exists and in which the everyday world must be made to participate. The criterion is there but hidden; the function of philosophy is to reveal the hidden form. The Royal Ruler has a dual function: to discern the form of justice and to interpret the everyday world in its light.

Here, too, Plato and Aristotle differ. The good does not function in this way in Aristotle and so is not a criterion of the Platonic kind. The fact that it is not has led to persistent criticism of its emptiness. Yet it is precisely its emptiness that is its strength. I do not want to suggest that Aristotle propounded exactly the version of criterion that I shall eventually recommend. But he does differ from Plato in exactly those places where another theory of criterion would require him to differ.

Prudence is the core of Aristotle's ethical theory. In this he differs from Plato in two equally important ways.

The first I have already mentioned: whereas Plato urges the following of a law since not to do so would result in totally random deviation from it, Aristotle acknowledges prudent judgment. The second difference is associated with the first: for Plato the good is abstract: what is truly just, truly good, is the form; for Aristotle, the good is concrete: the good is achieved in this act, in this situation, with these details. To make too sharp a contrast would be to dismiss Plato unfairly; in some, but not in all, respects, Plato's Royal Ruler is Aristotle's prudent man.

Aristotle's theory fits into his basic metaphysical structure of form and act. Because human living is a pattern of recurrent actions, where situations not only differ from one another but also resemble one another, it is possible to think of types or kinds of situation. We can ask what is to be done in such and such a kind of situation and can come up with an answer. The set of traditional answers to the set of traditional questions about the set of traditional recurring kinds of situation is the traditional ethic of a community.

War was a recurrent kind of situation, and so the question arose about how a soldier engaged in war was to behave and, in answer to that question, the idea of bravery arose. But the soldier is actually brave at a particular moment, and to know what is demanded at a particular moment is prudential. The soldier may be habitually brave. One discovers that a soldier is habitually brave by discovering that, on those actual individual occasions that call for bravery, he acts bravely rather than foolhardily or cowardly. So the habit of bravery demands both insight and decision. In the same way, one discovers that someone is habitually a good builder by discovering that, on those occasions when he is actually building, he builds well. Again, one discovers that someone is habitually just when one discovers that, whenever an occasion to be just in practice arises, the person acts justly. From this comes the definition of the virtue or habit of justice in Roman law as the constant and enduring disposition to give to each his due.

There is a virtue or habit of justice, only because there are recurrent situations within which the question as to what belongs to whom arises; there is a virtue or habit of bravery because war is a recurrent human situation; there is a virtue of building because houses are in recurrent demand. Were the political situation to change so radically that, quite literally, no situations occurred within which the question of what belonged to whom was relevant, then the virtue of justice would disappear, just as the virtue of building would disappear were there nothing to be built.

This may at first glance seem odd, for one may be inclined to think that the virtue of justice could emerge independently of the situation. I suggest that it could and would not, for there would be no need for it in a situation in which there were no goods to distribute or no possibility of transfers between people of goods that were in some sense theirs. The question of a just distribution arises because there are goods to be distributed and because a distributive practice has grown up. The question of rectifying an unjust situation arises only where there is a transfer of goods between people. In all known human communities both situations occur. There are communities where the idea of property and ownership is not that of eighteenth-century Europe, but there are no human communities where there exists no idea whatsoever of ownership, no distinction between what is mine, what is yours, what is ours.

One moves from being habitually just to being actually just only in a situation within which the question of what belongs to whom arises. In general, one moves from habit to act by asking the question, giving an answer, and acting in accord with the answer. The perennial objection to Aristotle at this point is, But how do you know what belongs to whom? Your definition is vacuous! Some version of this objection is put, in modern times, by both Kelsen and Perelman, among others.[10]

In fact, this is not really an objection. Aristotle's definition is not at all a criterion of this kind, and his answer to the objection is that you know what belongs to whom by investigating the situation. The objection is not powerful as an objection because it fails to grasp that the definition is not a Platonic criterion. Nonetheless, it is a real and important question.

How do we discover what belongs to whom? Sometimes the task is easy. Suppose that you find a wallet on the floor of a theater lobby. If you are habitually just, you will want to give it to its owner and so you will ask who the owner is. You cannot be actually just until you find the owner. Your next move will be to devise a strategy that will yield the answer to that question: perhaps you will have an announcement made, perhaps you will put up a notice, and so on. You may or may not succeed, but the central issue here is that you know how to go about finding the answer to what you know is the relevant question, Who owns this wallet? Your inquiry has, however, taken place within a social context that you have accepted. You have not, for example, raised any fundamental questions about the distribution of wealth in the community.

There are occasions when such fundamental questions should be raised but, once again, whether or not they are relevant is itself an ethical question. Leaving them aside for the moment, however, it is worth analyzing the simple example in greater detail.

First, why does a question arise at all? It is certainly possible to imagine a society in which the perfectly accepted rule was "finders keepers." In that society, the question as to who owned the wallet would not arise, simply because it had already been answered: the finder is the owner. One would no more ask a question about who owned the wallet than one would ask who owned a shell one found on the shore. Quite simply, the question arises because the situation of finding a wallet on the floor of a theatre is defined in our culture as one in which the question as to who owns it arises. If a small child finds it, one of the first things that a parent will say is that the owner must be found and the wallet given back. There is a crucial difference between the person who picks up the wallet and does not bother to try to discover its owner and the person who genuinely does not know that the question arises. The first person is unjust; the second person fails to understand what the social situation is.

Second, why does the question arise about a wallet but not always about a shirt button or a safety pin? The answer is so obvious that the question seems merely foolish. There is an understanding in our society that it is not usually worth doing anything about a shirt button or a safety pin or even a coin of little value. Once again the general point is that to know whether or not the question arises is part of understanding the social situation.

Third, when you find the wallet the actual social situation is one in which, as a matter of fact, you have what does not belong to you and the owner is deprived of it. Although no one is to blame, there is an unjust situation. The situation will be just when the wallet is returned to its owner. The way of moving from the unjust to the just situation is by asking the question as to who owns the wallet, answering it successfully, and restoring the wallet to its owner. The just is entirely concrete and individual, and the actual questions that need to be asked are very pedestrian.

Fourth, the achievement of the just situation is individual and concrete. It consists in restoring this wallet to this person. We do, however, understand the situation under the general rubric of restoring to people what belongs to them.

Fifth, the general rubric is general and the situation is particular. And so questions can arise about the appropriateness of restoring the wallet on this particular occasion. Because these questions can arise and because sometimes it may not be appropriate to restore the wallet, the general rubric should not be applied blindly to particular cases. Rather the general rubric is an aid to understanding the particular situation.

Sixth, should you try to discover who owns the wallet and give it back? Inasmuch as you understand the society it will occur to you that this is what is expected. You will realize that this is what you have been taught. You will realize that to achieve a just situation by restoring the wallet to its owner is not, in our culture, a neutral fact but a value. And so you may ask yourself whether or not it is a value you accept. This last question arises because if, at first, we learn our ethics as we learn our language, eventually we take, or may take, a personal stand. We may ask not only whether we are living up to our tradition, but whether, in the end, we find it acceptable.[11]

Finally, the movement from habit to act is central. It is in the act that the good is achieved. Corresponding to habit and act in the person are possibility and realization in the situation. For the situation in which ethical questions arise is one that may be other than it is and where change can be effected by human decision. We deliberate about a possible future that can be realized by our decisions. The good is the realized situation.

4. The extrinsic norm

In Plato the form is the criterion; the form is known by the Royal Ruler, whose knowledge is expressed in a law that itself becomes a criterion for those who do not see the form. A particular way of understanding Plato— or, as I think, misunderstanding Plato—is one source of Occamian ethical theory.

A second source is the Bible. The Bible does not propose an ethical theory, but theoretical reflection on it may well yield command theory.[12]

A third source is the opposition to St. Thomas Aquinas, whose work was condemned in 1277 in Paris shortly after his death, because his approach seemed to limit God's freedom by suggesting that God could not command anything whatsoever but only what was good.

The question as to whether what was commanded was good because commanded or commanded because good was not asked in the Old or New Testament, but it was, so to speak, there in embryo and was explicitly asked by the medieval theologians.

St. Thomas Aquinas's answer was unequivocal: if God commanded something, it was because what he commanded was good. Something that was bad could not be made good simply by virtue of being commanded by God.

This was thought by Aquinas's critics to limit God unacceptably and Occam appeared to extend God's freedom by allowing him to command everything but the contradictory. It is central to Occam that God could have commanded otherwise than he did and that what he did command is good only because he commanded it or bad only because he forbade it. In themselves acts are neutral.[13]

There are several important stories in the Old Testament that make Occam's position plausible as a theoretic account of the Hebrew ethic. Yahweh commanded Abraham to sacrifice Isaac. Therefore, killing one's son must be in itself neutral. For Occam, Abraham did not sin in being willing to follow Yahweh's command to kill Isaac. He was commanded to do so and so to kill Isaac would not have been sinful. In the Index to the B.A.C. edition to St. Thomas's *Summa Theologiae* we read, "Abraham being willing to kill Isaac, did not sin because he had to obey God's command." This is given as St. Thomas's solution to the problem, which it is not. It is, however, Occam's solution.

St. Thomas's solution is more difficult and, to modern readers, probably no more acceptable than it was to Occam. He treats the matter four times and his answers, although not identical on each occasion, are very similar. The fullest treatment is in the First Part of the Second Part of the *Summa Theologiae* (question 94, article 5, answer to the second objection). Article 5 asks whether the law of nature can be changed, and the second objection to the suggestion that it cannot be changed is that 'it is against the natural law to kill the innocent. . . but this is found to be changed by God as when He commanded Abraham to kill his innocent son as is recounted in Genesis 22.2" The relevant parts of the answer are worth giving in full:

> To the second objection it may be said that death comes naturally to us all, to the guilty and to the innocent. For natural death was introduced by God following original sin as appears from the 1 *Kings* 2,6: The Lord killeth and maketh alive. Accordingly, without any injustice, following a command of God, he may inflict death on anyone, whether guilty or innocent.

I think few modern readers will be persuaded by St. Thomas's answer. A modern exegesis would concentrate on the historicity of the Bible, but the important point here is not whether St. Thomas's answer is persuasive. The point is that he is not content to argue simply that God can command whatever he likes; God can command Abraham to kill Isaac because already death comes equally to the innocent and the guilty.

Both St. Thomas and Occam were faced with the same problem: how to reconcile what was apparently a sin with God's command. They solved the problem differently. Occam's solution is simpler than St. Thomas's and has been more influential, for with this theory he does two important things.

First, he places Christianity and the Bible squarely within command theory, and this has considerable significance for the subsequent religious and philosophical development of the West. Second, he opens the way to a long history of a particular kind of search for criteria.[14]

There is a third aspect to Occam that deserves mention. Although God could command what he wished and could have commanded otherwise, still, in practical affairs, where there were no evident commands from God, decisions clearly rested on the investigation of the situation. Thus the way is open for a division between the practical and the ethical that has had deleterious effects and that makes it difficult for modern readers to accept the delineation, suggested here, of the ethical field as the domain of deliberation and choice.

With Occam, God's command becomes the criterion of ethical action. In later thought, this tradition divides into three streams. First, there is the religious stream, where God's command remains the criterion. Martin Luther is, in this, Occam's disciple and the influence remains very clearly in Karl Barth and Jacques Ellul. Second, there is the secular stream, where the command of the Sovereign replaces the command of God. The great and enduring representative of this tradition is Thomas Hobbes, and it is through him that the Occamian tradition retains most of its power in modern philosophy. The clearest modern example is Hans Kelsen's *Pure Theory of Law*, where the basic norm, upon which all law rests, has the same structural position as Hobbes's Sovereign or Occam's God. The modern natural law tradition is the third stream, in which God's command becomes the innate moral law, conceived, clearly or confusedly, as a set of propositions. It is within this stream that ethics conceived as geometry with unassailable axioms is most at home. This tradition is often associated with Roman Catholic writers and so with St. Thomas. But it is with a St. Thomas read through the obscuring mirror of Occam.

In all three streams the criterion of action is propositional and external to the situation. Proponents of each version dispute with one another sometimes in a way that reveals their fundamental, if obscured, agreement. In *Table-Talk*, Hobbes's contemporary, John Selden, writes:

> I cannot fancy to myself what the Law of Nature means, but the Law of God. How should I know I ought not to steal, I ought not to commit Adultery, unless somebody had told me so?[15]

Clearly Selden conceives the law of God as a series of propositions—Thou shalt not steal; Thou shalt not commit adultery—and imagines that the law of nature must also be a series of propositions, perhaps the same propositions, indeed, but from a different source or, more exactly, differently from the same source, for, ultimately, the natural law theorists did, as a matter of fact, think that the innate natural law derived from God, as did all creation. Selden objects to natural law because he cannot conceive propositions' being innate. Hobbes's opponent, Coke, speaks of natural law's deriving from reason, but neither he nor anyone else was able to answer, or even to face squarely, Hobbes's simple question, Whose reason?[16]

In those few lines of Selden one can discern the central thrust of seventeenth-century ethical theory: to act well is to obey the commands of the lawgiver, for how else can one know what it is to act well? For Hobbes, the will of the Sovereign, expressed in law, is the criterion. Without law, there is the original state. Consequent is that if the Sovereign disappears, the law disappears and if the law disappears, there is no criterion of action.

Were there no merit in Occam's approach it would not have lasted over the centuries. It would not have been transformed into the positivist tradition. It would not have seemed, as it has seemed, to be the only rational account of ethical action. It is, therefore, necessary to discover precisely what questions it answers, or seems to answer, and why those questions seem important.

Common to all versions of this tradition is the question of the criterion of action. If actions are to be distinguished into good and bad, honorable and dishonorable, and so on, it is taken for granted that there must be some criterion. There are several candidates for the position of criterion—God's will, the will of the Sovereign, innate laws—but common is the idea of criterion. Common, too, is the conception of the criterion as a proposition, usually in the imperative mood.

None of this would be persuasive unless it seemed to account for how we actually behave. And, at least on first sight, it does so very well. Suppose I make the very ordinary ethical decision, I will stop writing now and begin again tomorrow morning. By making this decision I am choosing the rest of the evening without writing over some further time spent at my desk. I may not use the term *good* or *valuable*, but, in practice, I am choosing

an evening without writing as more valuable than one
spent writing. If this is a reasonable decision, then I
should be able to give a reason for it. If someone asks
me, "Why are you stopping now?" I may reply, "Because
I have been writing all day and am getting tired and
stale." But why is that a reason for stopping? I may go
on to say that if I am tired and stale I will not write
well. And my interlocutor may persist and ask why that
is a reason for stopping. At the end of this logical chain
there must be some unassailable proposition that is in
itself a reason and beyond which it is neither possible
nor necessary to go.

It seems to me that in everyday life we do in fact
have these, in practice unquestioned, propositions beyond which we find no need to go. So almost every
reader would, as a matter of fact, accept that being tired
and stale was a reason for stopping. The logical structure
of the practical argument then becomes something like
this:

> If I am tired and stale, I should stop.
> I am tired and stale.
> I should stop.

In everyday speech we do not usually bother to be quite
so formal and so we produce the enthymeme, or incomplete argument:

> I am tired and stale and should stop.

However, we expect the person to whom we are speaking
to understand that the argument is incomplete and to
supply the missing premise. We can rely on the person's
doing so because the missing premise is, in our culture,
so obvious as hardly to need articulation.

Our conversational partner may supply the missing
premise but may not accept it, and so we might attempt
to justify it:

> If I am going to write badly, I should stop.

> If I am tired and stale, I am going to write badly.
> If I am tired and stale, I should stop.

Once more, our conversational partner may reject either or both premises, in which case, as has been explicitly known and accepted since the dawn of logical analysis, we must find further premises from which the rejected premises may be concluded and so on until our companion accepts some basic premises without further argument.

This indefinitely expandable movement back to agreed premises, in practice comes to an end when the partners in a conversation, as a matter of fact, agree; when they have, in other words, discovered a shared context, defined by shared presuppositions.

Traditionally, however, this purely pragmatic agreement and sharing of context has been considered insufficient and, in place of basic premises that are as a matter of fact agreed, there are postulated either premises that are as a matter of principle agreed (various versions of modern natural law theory) or premises that are accepted on authority (various versions of command theory).

More recently there has emerged a third approach that suggests that the basic premises are culturally given. R. G. Collingwood calls these the absolute presuppositions of a culture, and, for him, metaphysics is the science that attempts to discover the basic presuppositions at work, but hardly articulated, in a culture. In Collingwood's analysis of the logic of question and answer, questions arise on presuppositions (for example, if I ask what your husband's name is, I am presupposing that you have a husband and that he has a name; if I ask for the Avogadro number of an element, I presuppose that elements have Avogadro numbers). Some presuppositions are themselves answers to earlier questions (for instance, the presupposition that you have a husband

is itself logically the answer to the question, Have you
a husband?) and those earlier questions likewise arise
on presuppositions. Finally, to prevent the infinite re-
gress of question and presupposition, Collingwood suggests that there must be absolute presuppositions that
are not the answers to questions but are simply presupposed. These absolute presuppositions are neither true
nor false but are, so to speak, ways of looking at the
world. They are neither true nor false because they are
not propositions but what Collingwood sometimes calls
working hypotheses. Collingwood is by no means the
only exponent of a theory of this kind but he is one
of the clearest. What remains important about his particular exposition is the clarity of its logic. Collingwood's
absolute presuppositions are in the same structural position as the earlier unassailable first principles.[17]

There is a sense in which the cultural tradition oc-
cupies the same logical place as Hobbes's Sovereign or
Occam's God since the culture becomes the authority
on which the presuppositions are accepted. But there
is, too, a clear and important difference. The cultural
tradition is not conceived as the product of a single
mind or coherent group of cooperating minds from
which rules emanate but as the product of a vast and
enduring practical cooperative interaction between people over centuries—what Hayek has called a *taxon*.

Collingwood was not entirely satisfied with his own
position. He knew that people could switch from one
set of absolute presuppositions to another set; he considered that such a switch was a momentous development in a culture or in an individual, but he was unable,
and recognized that he was unable, to give a satisfactory
account of it.

It is a commonplace to distinguish natural law theorists with their naturally known first principles conceived
as propositions, command theorists with their commands coming from some conception of God or Sov-

ereign, and relativists with their culturally shared basic presuppositions. But the central point of the present section is much less to distinguish between them than to show their identity. And their underyling identity consists in the operative but obscure assumption of logical system as the paradigm of human knowing and valuing. In other words, the fundamental criteria must be propositions or axioms or presuppositions whether these are naturally known, commanded, or culturally given and unquestionable.

I do not intend to minimize the important difference between proponents of the various approaches. The difference between the proponents of somehow naturally known unassailable propositions and the proponents of presuppositional relativity is both profound and important. Richard Rorty's well-known *Philosophy and the Mirror of Nature* is in many respects an analysis of the differences and an indication of how important they are and to what different conclusions they lead. Still, underneath the profound difference there is the even more profound, but concealed, agreement that I have tried to uncover.

5. Traditions and operations

The good is always totally concrete and specific. The good that is the object of deliberation and choice is initiated by the question, What will I (or we) do now? The internal goal of that practical question is the decision that realizes the good. When the questioner first raises the question, the good is intended but is not yet known. The questioner moves from intended but unspecified good to specifying the good and deciding to realize it. In the passage from original intention, through specification, to eventual realization, commonly enough several possible specifications are invented and considered; for the present, within which the questioner stands, is rarely, if ever, open only to a single possibility. There can then arise a question of deciding between possibilities but, of course, only between those possibilities that have occurred to the questioner. As in a game of chess, of all the abstractly possible moves, only those that a player actually notices at the time are genuine possibilities of that particular game as it is being played.

These are practical, indeed everyday, questions. Everyone is engaged constantly in this specification and realization of the good. Will I return the telephone call now or after my meeting? Will I cook spinach or carrots for dinner? Will we get married? Will I take early retirement? What will I do about the famine in Ethiopia? What will I do about the rise of drug-related crime? Will we legalize some now proscribed drugs? Will we proscribe some now legal drugs? Will we take a summer holiday? How large an allowance will we give our daughter? Will we buy a new or secondhand car? Will I learn Norwegian? Will I study mathematics or archaeology? Will I become intensely involved in the opposition to the government's foreign policy? The list could go on indefinitely and readers will be able easily to make their own.

Sometimes these practical questions are easy to answer; sometimes they are not. Sometimes the possibilities chosen realize a world that many would suppose to be minimally different from the world that would have been produced had some other possibility been selected. Thus, few readers will suppose that the choice of carrots or spinach is usually of as much significance as the choice for or against marriage. When the question is easy, we answer it easily; indeed, we say that the question is easy precisely because we find it usually easy to answer. But sometimes the question is hard and then we tend to seek criteria more explicitly.

Up to now I have suggested that the search for criteria has been undertaken with a logical image of human knowing. I have distinguished three streams within the inquiry. In this chapter I shall deal with criteria under two main headings with a logical interlude: (5.1) Tradition, (5.2) A Logical Interlude, and (5.3) Operations. Also, although this will become clear only in the section on operations, I shall present and undertake the inquiry with an idea of human knowing and valuing as other than logical system.

5.1 Traditions

Whatever is present but has not been discovered by the presently living members of a community is traditional. More colorfully, and also more accurately, whatever is present at a given moment, artificially halted in conception, is traditional. We can in principle know the state of the English language on 10 August 1988 by taking as our data all current expressions until but not beyond that date. We can know what is traditional in physics on the same date by knowing what is held in contemporary physics until but not beyond that date. We can know the traditional ethics of a community by discovering the values of a community at a given time. Studies with such titles as "German Painting in the Fifteenth Century," and "Twentieth-Century Physics" are analyses of traditions.

The terms *tradition* and *traditional* are not always used in this way. When traditional physics is mentioned, the speakers often mean Newtonian physics, or nonquantum physics. When traditional farming is mentioned, the speakers may mean plowing with a horse, or using only organic manure, and so on. By traditional ethics may be meant what was, or was imagined to be, the set of values of an earlier time. In general, then, this usage introduces some more or less arbitrary watershed between the "traditional" and the modern. Quite frequently, there is a gentle irony in this use of the word for what is referred to as traditional is not at all what is handed down but much more what used to be handed down and no longer is. For everyday conversation this usage may well be unexceptionable, but it is inadequate for analysis and the terms are not used in this way here.

Contemporary physics is not stagnant and so new discoveries are being added to the tradition, to correct or refine it, and themselves become part of it, somewhat as new usages are added to a living language or as new paintings are added to the corpus of painting. Sometimes the new discoveries so radically correct the tradition that historians can speak of radical breaks and revolutionary science; sometimes the discoveries simply refine and develop in a more ordered or acceptable way and slowly prepare the next radical step, which is never a random break but an insightful resolution of strains, present and more or less clearly known, in the science of the day.[18]

The apprentice physicist learns the physics of the day, that is, learns the tradition, in the hope of developing it either normally or radically. However, to learn the tradition is neither easy nor automatic and as learning is a prerequisite for development, failure to learn may lead to decline. What was once understood may be understood no longer; careful assessment of hypotheses may yield to slovenly practice; the desire to learn may be subverted by various political pressures. Decline as much as development is possible.[19]

The apprentice physicist learns the tradition; learns, not nature, but physics; learns, not what infallibly is so, but the best available opinion of the day. The tradition is the starting point and the tradition is the physics of the day.

The ethical tradition is the ethic of the day: a collection of evaluations. The collection is not necessarily internally coherent even within a homogeneous and slowly changing culture. In a heterogeneous and rapidly changing culture the likelihood of coherence within the collection is remote and, in modern Western culture, is absent. What children learn when they learn an ethical tradition is a collection of evaluations about recurrent actions in the society: what is lovable, what detestable, what honorable, what just, what important, what ephemeral, what polite, what rude, what is in good or bad taste and so, more or less indefinitely, on. They learn not only the content of the classification but the classification itself; not only what is honorable and what is dishonorable but the classifying pair "honorable-dishonorable." Just as the content of a classification may change or may differ from community to community so too may the classification itself come into prominence or fall into desuetude. The classification "honorable-dishonorable" is, I suspect, much less prominent in modern Western civilization than it used be; it is probably more in evidence in some parts of the culture than in others. Whether the young child learns the classification and learns to distinguish actions into honorable and dishonorable depends on place of birth, class, and so on. The classifying pair "honorable-dishonorable" is cultural. Children learn the tradition in a variety of ways: from the significant surrounding adults, from their peers, from nursery rhymes and childrens' stories, from their older siblings, from the artistic expressions current in the culture—television dramas, advertisements, news presentations; from schools and churches, and so on. In a relatively simple homogeneous slowly changing small society, not only the content but the sources of the ethical tradition are homogeneous. In modern Western society heterogeneity is everywhere.

No child in a modern state is now brought up in a coherent ethical tradition, and some elements in the tradition respond to its heterogeneity so what is presented by one source as valuable may, quite deliberately, and in opposition, be presented by another source as valueless or more or less irrelevant.

The ethical tradition is pervasive, including the enormously significant and the trivial. It introduces the child into a world of values and does so dominantly through an education of feeling. These values are not necessarily the values that the child will adopt and live with during an entire life, but they are the values that he or she finds are his or her own in somewhat the same way as a native language. As the child gradually and more or less clearly and decisively becomes autonomous, he or she does so through the ethic of the society and finds that further autonomous development is, and must be, from this cultural beginning.[20]

Values are not one's own as if they were something beside oneself; they are oneself. They are at any moment what one is, even if one is open to being something else. Perhaps the ethical tradition that, in recent years, has most clearly in practice recognized value as identification is the feminist. Many feminist writers clearly see that adult women are not value-neutral beings who happen to have a set of values tacked on that they can easily discard in favor of another set; they recognize that adult women are these values and that any proposed change is at once radical and painful. Men are equally their values and, in this area, their values are correlative of the women's. The changes advocated within the feminist tradition very clearly demand a change in what men and women are. Inasmuch as women change while men do not, an earlier cultural coherence is dislocated and a new coherence has yet to be achieved. Just as quantum mechanics developed from acknowledged strains within its tradition, so too, feminism grew from strains brought about by shifts in technology, economy, and polity as much as by new developments in other areas of thought.

The ethical tradition is expressed directly in actions and in responses to action. To that extent the tradition is simply what is done and so is completely specific. But inasmuch as the tradition is expressed in stories, songs, advertisements, proverbs, laws, and so on, it is necessarily general or typical. The tradition as it is expressed in various rhetorical formulations tends to highlight and select. If this typical expression acts as a criterion of particular actions we have still to ask how it does so.

Consider the Fourth Commandment of the Decalogue: "Honor thy father and thy mother." In Deuteronomy the command appears thus:

Honor thy father and thy mother, as Yahweh, thy God, has commanded thee, that thou mayest have long life and mayest prosper in the land that Yahweh, thy God, gives to thee.

Both expressions are clearly versions of what is in some sense the same tradition, but they are not at all identical. The deuteronomical text associates honoring one's parents not only with obeying God—the shorter version does this insofar as the text is accepted as one of God's commandments—but also with having long life, prosperity, and the promised land. None of this remains in the shorter version, where the context of the Commandments within Christianity is the ethical life linked to eternal reward. In Christianity, too, as in later Judaism, the idea of desert and entitlement changes. As Western culture becomes more heterogeneous and secular, agnostic or atheistic imagery competes with religious, the link with obedience to God declines or disappears altogether. And yet the idea that parents are entitled to something from their children has not wholly gone. Something like the injunction to honor one's parents remains, however it is expressed.[21]

How, then, does the commandment influence action? It is at once obvious that the command cannot be obeyed if one does not know what "honor" means. It is only slightly less obvious that it cannot be obeyed if one does not know what "thy father and thy mother" means.

What does "honor" mean? This is the kind of question that Socrates put to the young men of Athens and too rapidly concluded that, because they could not define the term, they did not know what honor involved. But Plato, through Socrates, made another and, perhaps more far-reaching and influential, mistake. Because he thought that one would know honor by knowing the abstract and immutable form "honor," he, at least implicitly, thought of honor or the like as being ideally the same for all societies at all times.

It is clear from the dialogues that Plato knew how his compatriots tried to answer the question, What is

honor? They gave examples of honorable behavior or of
the kind of thing that would count as honorable. They
knew what honor was by being able to enumerate examples, and this knowledge helped them recognize honorable behavior when they came across it. And is not
this what we should spontaneously do if we were asked
to define "honor"? As the child grows up, this is how
the value of honor is communicated. Perhaps in a community honoring one's father and mother involves not
sitting down while they are standing. The child learns
this by, perhaps, being told to stand up when his mother
comes near. The visiting anthropologist learns this by
observing and discussing such behavior. Gradually the
anthropologist builds up, for another society, a picture
of what is meant by honor in the society being studied.
The anthropologist does for the society what, at least
in part, Aristotle did for the society of his time in the
Nicomachean Ethics. (The *Nicomachean Ethics* is not simply an anthropological monograph but it is that as
well.)[22]

In the ethical tradition into which I was born, men
honored women by standing up when a woman entered
a room in which the man was sitting, by giving a woman
his seat in a bus or train, by walking on the woman's
left or on the outside of the sidewalk. Are those actions
still part of honoring? Certainly so? Questionably so?
Certainly not? Or is the whole idea of men's honoring
women gone? Or does it exist in some modern traditions
and not in others? What can happen, and what I suspect
has happened, is that some actions once considered as
honoring now are considered as surreptitiously dishon-
oring women. Such a change can come about when a
great change in the relations between the sexes in a
culture comes about and the older forms seem now to
be an unacceptable insistence on the obsolete relation.
And yet the notion of honor, obscure and inarticulate,
may survive, not because we have some dark glimpse

of the Platonic form of honor but because we have a
practical and tentative understanding of the relevance
in our practice of the distinction between honor and
dishonor. The classification is the beginning of a perception of the social universe. That practical and tentative understanding is constantly being developed, criticized, radically changed.

The tradition provides a context, but it does not and
cannot specify precisely what is involved for this person
at this time in this situation with these parents. That
specification of the culture must be left to the individual,
who will do it well or badly, generously or meanly, and
so on.

There is, then, a real question about what honoring
involves but there is also a quite different question: Why
should I honor my parents? There are two very different
answers. The first is, because it is commanded or because
it is traditional. This answer will, sooner or later, evoke
the further question as to why one should obey the
commandment or follow the tradition. The second answer is very different: because it is valuable. And this
answer evokes two questions: Why is it valuable? and
How do I discover that it is?

Obviously, we first discover that it is valuable because
the tradition so instructs us. We may ask questions
about our tradition but we have it first. We are, as a
matter of fact, believers in our tradition and it is from
that belief that we must begin our inquiry.[23]

The ethical tradition is not here very different from
the scientific tradition. The apprentice physicist believes
in the tradition of physics and it is from there that
development takes place. We may as babies begin as
blank sheets, but when we begin to take responsibility
for our lives the sheets are already well written on.

We can, however, ask the other question: Why is to
honor one's parents valuable? It is simply not an answer
to this question to say that it is valuable because the

tradition says so just as it is no answer to say that Coulomb's law is true because Coulomb said so and physicists continue to think so.

It will not be thought sufficient merely to assert, as I have done, that a particular answer is not an answer, particularly since the rejected suggestion is one that has appeared in various guises in Western philosophy. It will be necessary to deal with this more directly later, but first I shall try to put forward another and, I think, more adequate answer to the question.

The question, then, is, Why is to honor one's parents valuable? The Western tradition suggests that it is and the first reason why the question arises at all is precisely that the tradition puts forward this value; we ask about the value because the value already exists in the culture. The answer that I shall suggest can be briefly formulated and must then be elaborated. The injunction to honor father and mother is formulated in the tradition because it was once discovered that this was a value and, further, thought valuable to express this discovery in a culturally significant rhetorical form. Similarly, Coulomb formulated his law in the 1780s and communicated his discovery in culturally significant rhetorical forms—in his case, scientific papers—in 1788 and 1789. The ethical community of which we are a part has not so far repudiated this discovery just as, so far, physicists have not rejected Coulomb's law.[24]

What has been discovered once can be discovered again, and so we may develop more authentically within our own tradition by attempting such a rediscovery. We may make the attempt by an interpretive, historical, and dialectical study of the tradition. In the present case we might begin by examining the idea of honor in the Bible and in subsequent writings very directly related to the Bible; we might continue by studying historical changes and continuities in the meaning and place of honor within Western civilization. We should assume as

a working hypothesis that honor in early Hebrew no-
madic society is unlikely to be the same as honor in
modern Irish cities, which, in its turn, is unlikely to be
the same as honor among modern Greek mountain
farmers nor as honor in eighteenth-century France. We
might discern fundamental differences in attitude behind distinct manifestations of honor, but all the while
we would be trying to discover the character of that
social relation that, in Western civilization, has been
classified as honor. Along the way we would make
explicit what was already obscurely and in practice felt
to be so, namely that ethical terms like *honor* have not
the same distinct and settled meaning as have the
technical terms of a science.

To restrict our inquiry to such a literary investigation
would, of course, be excessively narrow. Indeed, the
implicit suggestion that such a scholarly pursuit would
be the first step is, perhaps, more indicative of the
background and context of the author of this essay than
of anything else. We could equally well look for examples
of well thought of relationships between parents and
their children. More significantly still, we might examine
our own relations with our parents to discover strains
and imperfections. It is difficult but not impossible to
deepen our understanding of honor in general and of
honor between parents and children in specific.

In a society where honor is a central value why is to
honor one's parents valuable? We do not in fact live in
a Hobbesian world. Our first contact with others is
neither contract nor aggression. There is a mass of
obscured responses studied by psychoanalysis. There is,
too, a spontaneous affection that is ordered differently
in different societies, and in many societies—the over-
whelming majority if not all—the initial intersubjective
affectivity among father, mother, and offspring is taken
up in the social order. It is not always taken up in the
same way. In many parts of Africa the mother's brother

is at least as important as the father. Where the initial intersubjective relations are taken up into the order, then, as the child grows up, these adults remain important and the question of the relation between the adult offspring and parents arises. It is not a relation that occurs in isolation but within a complex network of other relations. Still, as a matter of social fact, the presence of parents is different from the presence of other adults of their generation. To honor someone is to acknowledge his position, his status, his being in relation to oneself. It is to hold that person in some esteem. Reasons for esteem are many and various, but one reason may be simply the person's role or position: the person is honored as being in that position. When one begins to examine the social situation it seems reasonable to honor one's parents.

Some features of the analysis are worth examining more closely. I am not suggesting that the commandment to honor father and mother is somehow applied out of the blue to any society whatsoever. I mentioned that the mother's brother is, in many parts of Africa, as significant as, or more significant than, the father. In such societies, it is more likely that the mother's brother will be singled out for honor. What I am trying to suggest is that, in a society where honor is a central theme, where children are cared for centrally by their fathers and mothers, where there exists a relation of respect between the generations, it is reasonable to single out parents for honor.

The story of Moses' bringing the Ten Commandments, inscribed on tablets of stone, from the mountain, after his encounter with Yahweh is well known. It is, or has been, one of the crucial foundation stories of Jewish, Christian, and, therefore, Western civilization.[25] Foundation stories are meditated upon throughout the ages and a dominant mode of reception emerges. The story of Moses has been received as a prime symbol of

God's commanding His creatures. Within Christianity, and, therefore, within Western civilization more generally, the story of Moses has to some extent eclipsed the earlier foundation story of Abraham. With the rise of Occam's theory of the good as what is commanded and the secularization of this in Hobbes, the image of Moses' bringing Yahweh's Commandments and imposing them on a society to which they were totally alien has, almost unbeknown to us, influenced our thinking. There are some features in the story as it is told in Deuteronomy and elsewhere that can reinforce this image. Further reinforcement comes from reading the story of Moses as history.

But if we try to break for a moment with that image and look at the story from an anthropological or literary critical perspective, it will at once strike us that it is inconceivable that the Commandments of the Decalogue were unknown to the people to whom Moses brought them. There is nothing new in the Decalogue. The Commandments are obviously simply some of the more important of those laws that the community considered central to its understanding of itself.[26]

Throughout the world, one finds that those laws that a community considers central to its understanding of itself are expressed in foundational stories that account for the origin of the laws, for their importance and for the most important fact that they are greater than the people who inherit them. The foundation stories make the basic laws invulnerable. Sophocles' *Antigone* is the dramatic presentation of a conflict between the eternal, invulnerable laws handed down by the gods to the ancestors and the laws imposed by the ruler, Creon. *Antigone* has many themes but one is certainly the end of invulnerability.

Our dominant image of a law is that it is an instruction from a sovereign to a subject. The subject is imagined as fully formed, simply waiting for the instruction to do this or that. This image lies behind Occam's idea that God could have commanded otherwise, and behind Hobbes's idea that the actions that proceed from the passions are no sin "till they know a Law which forbids them: which till the Lawes be made they cannot know: nor can any Law be made, till they have agreed upon the Person that shall make it" (*Leviathan*, chap. 13). Many archaic societies treat their laws not simply as commands, which might have been otherwise, but as definitions of themselves. So, in the story of Moses, there is the rhetoric of command; this occurs within the encompassing rhetoric of the dialogue between Yahweh and Moses that recalls Abraham and, therefore, the covenant that is the fundamental defining image.

I have been suggesting that the injunction to honor father and mother is the answer to a question about social relations that arises within a particular society. I shall turn now to a different but related example to illustrate more clearly the kind of answer I have been proposing. In modern Western society parents often ask how they are to treat their adolescent children. We ask this for a number of reasons, some of which are set down here:

First, we ask because we have adolescent children; we live in a society in which, for the most part, our offspring remain under our guardianship and financial dependence during their adolescence and often young adulthood; were this not the case, the question would arise differently.

Second, we ask because we sometimes find that the shift from childhood to adolescence leaves us with a set of parental habits or virtues that are not appropriate to the changed situation; the new or changed situation is the shift from childhood to adolescence and this is the source of new questions.

Third, we ask not only ourselves but friends and experts because we assume that others have gone

through a similar situation and that their solutions may
be helpful.

In every human society there is a development from
childhood to adulthood; in every human society the
difference between childhood and adulthood is noticed,
but this does not mean that the pertinent questions in
different societies are in every respect the same. We
should not ask the questions about adolescence that we
do in fact ask had we no adolescent children or had we
none in the way that we do in fact have them. Nor
should we ask those questions if we automatically, and
quite without difficulty, switched from one set of virtues
or habits appropriate to one situation to another set of
virtues appropriate to another situation. We should not
read books on the question did we feel that our personal
experiences were in every single respect unique.

In every human society there is a development from
childhood to adulthood. I am suggesting, therefore, that,
in every society, there is a set of parental virtues or
habits appropriate to the parent-child relation and another set of parental virtues or habits appropriate to
the parent-adult-offspring relation. It should by now be
wholly obvious that there is absolutely no suggestion
that the habits or virtues appropriate to one society are
necessarily appropriate to another. Insofar as the situations resemble one another, then it is likely enough that
the appropriate virtues or habits will resemble one another. Insofar as situations differ, then the appropriate
habits or virtues will correspondingly differ.

The habits or virtues agreed to be appropriate are
the practical solutions to practical problems within that
society. Laws express these solutions in a general or
typical way. Laws may well be commands; they may
well be expressed in the imperative mood; but they are
also the typical expressions of culturally acceptable solutions to recurrent practical situations. Thus, laws express the tradition.

In societies where the pattern of social life has been only very slowly changing over the centuries, we may expect to find solutions elaborated, generally known, and generally accepted. So, in many archaic societies, the passage from childhood to adulthood was marked by very carefully elaborated, universally known and accepted rituals and, often, tests. Among the Ngatatjara of central Australia the young man was sent into the desert alone to fend, for some months, for himself. Nowadays, among those Ngatatjara who still live in the desert, the young man is sent away for some time to work in one of the towns that fringe the desert to the south. This testing time is given greater importance by its surrounding ritual of circumcision and the young man's introduction to the foundation stories and sites of his group. When the young man returns he is a young adult male, no longer a child, and he puts away, in a fairly formal manner, the things of childhood. There has occurred a shift in the pattern of relations and a shift in the appropriate virtues.

How the test is to take place, what the rituals are, how the young adult is to behave in his new status toward others and they to him: all these form part of what the Ngatatjara call, in English, their law.

In this brief discussion of adolescence in our society I may have seemed to be placing the treatment of adolescent children on the same footing as the Fourth Commandment. It is best to admit roundly that this is what I intend. I am placing the question of how to treat adolescent children on the same footing as the question of how to treat parents. Both questions seem to me to ask about the relations between members of a family in a society where the order takes up and institutionalizes the biological and intersubjective relations among father, mother, and offspring. This means, of course, that I take the question of how to treat adolescent children as a moral or ethical question.

The discussion of Ngatatjara practice is intended to show why the bringing together of the two questions may not be quite so bizarre as the reader may initially feel.

In the light of this discussion we may return briefly to "honor" and its elaboration.

Is it possible to formulate a law about how we should treat adolescent children? Perhaps the following would make a beginning:

> Thou shalt respect the emerging adulthood of thy adolescent children.

A likely objection to this formulation would be that it is empty; we do not know what "respect the emerging adulthood" means and so we do not know how to go about the task. It is quite true, and has been said in the earlier discussion of the Fourth Commandment of the Decalogue, that if one genuinely does not know—in any sense of know whatsoever—what "respect" means, then the formulation is indeed empty and useless.

But this is not, in fact, the case. Suppose a formulation had been passed down through the generations that read:

> Thou shalt _____ the emerging adulthood of thy adolescent children.

The recipients of the tradition would know only that their ancestors had thought the relation between parents and adolescent children sufficiently important to formulate their attitude on the issue. But the descendants would not know, from the formula, what that attitude was. When we replace the blank in the second formula with the term *respect* and so return to the original, we are not, as a matter of fact, faced with a meaningless term. We have some idea of what *respect* means, just as the Athenians had some idea of the meaning of their ethical terms.

The formulation is not empty nor is it fully specified. We must now face squarely the question that we have been skirting around: how are these nonempty yet not fully specified ethical terms understood? Plato's approach, which has been discussed already, was to claim that the term was understood and the activity to which the term referred was understood when the form was understood. So to understand the nature of the activity that we name *respect* one had to have a vision of the Form of Respect. I have thus far taken an interpretive and historical approach. We discover the meaning of the term *respect* and what is meant by respect in a given society by discovering how the term is used and examining the activities that are commonly called respectful. I have suggested that this is how the child learns the culture. That answer must now be enlarged.

I have sketched what is involved in the interpretive and historical approach. The interpreter deals with the relevant data from the community at a particular time and composes a monograph on the meaning of respect among that particular people at that period. The historian recognizes that what is, in some sense, the same community changes over time and through the generations and, having considered the meaning of respect at one time, at a second time, and a third time, and so forth, eventually produces a study of the development of the meaning of respect among that people over time and generations. As these studies proceed it may be noticed that there are not only coherence, agreement, and ordered development but also disagreement, radical shifts in approach; not only continuities but breaks. There emerges the need for a further study that, to interpretation and history, adds a study of basic differences.

What scholars attempt carefully, slowly, and tentatively, practical people—which all of us are some of the time or in some areas—attempt rapidly and incoherently.

They talk of, say, "Victorian values" or "liberal values" with the benefit of bits and pieces of folk memory, assorted books and articles, the rhetoric of the opinion makers of the day, and political interest. They may vaguely recognize shifts in values but tend to think, depending on their political attitudes, that the values they hold were always held or, alternatively, that the values they hold were never held and their position represents an enlightened leap from the benighted past. They recognize, more or less accurately, present radical differences of opinion but rarely attempt to trace them carefully to their source. They do so not only because they are not scholars but because their interests are different. The proper interest of practical people is what to do now, not what was done once, and it is this, not the scholarly interest, however much scholarship may illumine, that is the proper ethical interest. For the ethical question is, What is to be done now?

There is a pseudohistorical question about what a historical character would have done had another situation arisen. The question is pseudohistorical, although sometimes found in historical writing, because the answer cannot be known. Still, that pseudoquestion points to a further element in the understanding of respect.

Someone trying to respect the emerging adulthood of his adolescent children has a background understanding that he has from his tradition (his tradition, of course, includes his entire life until that moment; it is not something outside him), but his present question is, How do I respect the emerging adulthood of this particular person in this particular situation? He will rarely find his tradition totally unhelpful, but he will often find it insufficient. The tradition will not act as a sharply delineated criterion that he can, more or less automatically, apply to this new and unforeseen circumstance; it is much more like a field of action within which the detailed action must be invented. And so the inquirer may try to imagine how a respected figure would act in these circumstances. In Christian ethical practice, for example, the believer is sometimes asked to act as Christ would have acted, something that simply cannot be known historically but that can, nonetheless, play a part in the person's concrete ethical rhetoric.[27] Further analysis of the invention of the detailed action will be attempted in the section on operations that follows.

What is the source of the formulation "Thou shalt respect the emergent adulthood of thy adolescent children"? In an obvious sense, I have simply invented it by modeling it on the rhetorical form of a Commandment of the Decalogue. However, I suspect that most readers will have accepted it as a reasonable formulation of the attitude to adolescence in modern Western culture. Had I instead produced the formulation

Thou shalt jeer at the emerging adulthood of thy adolescent children.

I suspect that most readers would have recognized the rhetorical form of the command but would not have accepted the formulation as expressive of an appropriate attitude.

The formulation, then, expresses what is, in our society, taken to be an appropriate attitude. And what is the source of the attitude? There is a circular movement here. Initially, the attitude is a suggested answer to the practical question of how parents should deal with their growing children. But once the attitude is discovered and formulated, whether succinctly as in the present formula or diffusely in conversations, books, plays, advertisements, and so on, the traditional formulation in its turn educates into the tradition so that when parents are actually faced with the issue, the tradition already suggests the grand lines of the solution.

What has been discovered once can, in principle, be discovered again. Why, then, bother to enshrine the discovery in a tradition? Why not attempt to have everyone make the attempt at discovery himself or herself? The question calls eventually for a longer answer than will be provided here. The general answer is that humans find it valuable to communicate their discoveries and it is on this complex communication that human civilization is built. Without it there would be "no Knowledge of the face of the Earth; no account of Time; no Arts; no Letters; no Society. And the life of man, solitary, poore, nasty, brutish, and short" as Hobbes, in an apparently very different but in reality very similar context, so beautifully wrote.[28] An illustration may be helpful. When a child goes to school she begins to learn mathematics, but what she learns is not mathematics in the abstract but what is understood in her community to be mathematics. She is not asked to reinvent mathematics. Ramanujan, while a clerk on the Indian railway, stumbled across a book of algebra. He became fascinated by it and went on to rediscover many important theorems. He came to the notice of Hardy, who invited him to Cambridge. Ramanujan was a great mathematician. But he added almost nothing to mathematics simply because he began, poignantly, at the wrong place. As there is human cooperation and belief in mathematics, in the natural sciences, in painting and poetry, so also there is human cooperation and belief in ethics.

Because the natural sciences are popularly considered to be wholly "rational" and, so to speak, wholly reinvented in the mind of the individual scientist, the idea that they are traditional in the present sense may not find immediate acceptance. A specific example may clarify the claim. Among those studying gravity at the moment there is controversy about the existence of a so-called fifth force. Since Newton, the form of the law of gravity has been "1 over r squared" ($1/r^2$) with a constant G to be specified. By the Cavendish experiment in the early eighteenth century this relation was shown to hold over very small distances. Newton had suggested that it held at the astronomical level and this has been held ever since. The distances involved in the Cavendish experiment are very small (less than ten centimeters) relative to astronomical observations with distances of 96 million miles and more. For technical reasons it has been difficult to perform reliable experiments at intermediate distances. However, some recent experiments and recent reinterpretations of earlier experiments, with some claim to greater reliability, have yielded experimental results that deviate from those anticipated by the inverse square law. Some physicists, therefore, postulate an intermediate force distinct from gravity. More reject the suggestion.

I have neither wish nor competence to adjudicate among physicists. The point of the example is quite different and is simply this: the entire dispute is taking place within a long and complex tradition that we denote by the term *physics* and makes no sense outside that tradition. Outside that tradition the questions would simply not arise. A feature of the experiments within the controversy is that experimenters go down mine shafts and drop objects, but dropping objects underground is a completely ordinary activity when considered by itself and gains relevance and importance only when associated with the tradition of physics. The experimenters are not simply dropping objects: they are asking questions of the world.

In practical affairs, no less than in science, we begin from our tradition since our tradition is not only where but, more profoundly, what we are.

The attitude that I have formulated in the command to respect the emerging adulthood of adolescents is based on the human discovery that such respect is valuable. The discovery is, I think, true. But it is not infallible.

Neither is it complete. We have much yet to learn about the nature of the respect for emerging adulthood appropriate within the various streams of modern Western civilization.

I have used the vague phrase that the attitude to adolescence emerges in the culture in answer to a practical problem that has emerged in the culture. That vague answer will not do, but before trying to make it more precise, it is worth recalling the lines from Selden quoted previously:

> How should I know I ought not to steal, I ought not to commit Adultery, unless somebody had told me so?

The initial plausibility of Selden's position rests entirely on the fact that his contemporaries, and, to some extent, we, live in a culture where the story of Moses is a well-known foundational myth and where his examples are taken from that source. As that foundational myth fades into "the smooth permanence of ancient forms" the rhetorical power of writings that depend upon it will be, inevitably, transformed.

But, even where that myth still has force, were I to suggest that we should have no idea of how to treat our adolescent children unless somebody had told us so, almost every reader would strenuously resist. It is perfectly plain that the approved attitude toward adolescent children in our civilization comes neither from God nor from a secular lawgiver in the paradigm shared by Occam, Selden, Hobbes, and Kelsen. Most readers would at once repudiate, as merely silly, the idea that the way we treat our adolescent children is a matter of sheer indifference until some law about the matter is properly enacted.

Does modern natural law theory fare any better as an account of our attitude? Is it any more plausible to suggest that we know some innate principle, conceived as a proposition, that informs us how to treat adolescents or from which the correct way of treating adolescents may be deduced? And further, is it any more plausible to suggest that there is some such innate principle, conceived as a proposition, that informs us about honoring parents while failing to inform us about adolescent children?

I have presented an ethical tradition as the accumulation of wisdom in a society over generations; as communally suggested, and, often, communally accepted, answers to recurrent kinds of ethical questions; as the communally accepted way of dealing with recurrent situations. The ethical tradition is present in a community as its scientific tradition is present. In homogeneous societies the tradition is homogeneous; indeed, for a society to be homogeneous is for it to have a homogeneous tradition, for its members to share common concerns, to accept common solutions, to honor common values and aspirations. Where the society is heterogeneous, so also is the tradition, for heterogeneity means that the members, in some significant way, do not share concerns, solutions, goals, and values.

5.2 A logical interlude

I have suggested that we discover how to treat our parents or our adolescent children by examining our social situation, our communal lives. I seem, against Hume, to be deriving an "ought" from an "is."

Hume, writing of the practical syllogism, asserted, quite correctly, that if "ought" did not occur in the premises, then it could not validly occur in the conclusion. This Humean assertion is correct, clear, and important. However, on a purely historical note, it should be said that no philosopher prior to Hume thought otherwise. The version of the practical syllogism pre-

sented by Aristotle and by Aquinas has "ought," or
some logical equivalent, in the premises.[29]

In the instances of practical syllogisms given earlier,
some logical equivalent of "ought" very explicitly occurs
in the premises:

> If I am tired and stale, I *should* stop.
> I am tired and stale.
> I *should* stop.

> If I am going to write badly, I *should* stop.
> If I am tired and stale, I am going to write badly.
> If I am tired and stale, I *should* stop.

It should be fully accepted that, within the practical
syllogism, Hume's clarificatory point is perfectly correct.

On the other hand, I have presented an ethical
suggestion (an "ought") as a solution to a practical
question that arises in a concrete situation. And if I am
not to discover what I am to do in a concrete situation,
how else am I to make the discovery? The concrete
situation in which I find myself does, of course, include
me. There is no question of my being over against the
situation that is not me. The naive version of epistemological objectivity in which the subject is over against
the object—the term *object* understood etymologically as
"that which is thrown in front of"—spills over into
practical inquiry with equally disastrous results.

A specific ethical question—What will I do now in
these circumstances?—anticipates the specific ethical answer: I will do X. Traditional answers are not specific
in this way. They suggest typical ways of dealing with
typical situations and form the background within which
the ethical actor operates. If, quite radically, no one
human situation were ever, in any sense or to any extent,
like another human situation, then traditional answers
would be useless and patently so.

Hume's assertion can now be extended to mean that
by merely observing the actual social situation, one

cannot know what is to be done. And this, too, is totally correct. The situation does not yield an answer; the situation is simply the raw material or data upon which the question arises. The situation is that upon which the ethical actor operates.

What, then, is the source of the "ought"? We are. It is the sign, in the practical syllogism, of our grasp of ourselves as beings responsible for our own future and for the future of our world. It is the sign of our grasp of the present situation as a field of possibility, ordered toward a future for which we are, in part, responsible.[30]

5.3 Operations

Real ethical traditions are rarely totally systematic. They are collections of accumulated wisdom. It is, on the other hand, possible to make the attempt to systematize a tradition: the codification of law is an example of such an attempt.[31]

It is also possible to imagine that ethical tradition is logical system: that is, a set of propositions distinguished into definitions, postulates, and conclusions. If a tradition is imagined or conceived in this way, then it follows that there will be postulates within the tradition that are not demonstrable within it. Different traditions with different and incompatible postulates will be incommensurable, just as different geometries with mutually incompatible postulates are incommensurable. It further follows that if human responsibility is confined within a logical system, then insofar as there are incompatible logical systems there will be a radical relativism of traditions.

Suppose that there were two traditions, A and B. Both are logical systems with postulates, definitions, and conclusions. The ethical actors act wholly within one or other of the traditions. Suppose that a postulate of

A were, There can be no circumstances in which it would be good that an ethical actor stated what he or she knew to be untrue. Suppose that it were a postulate of B: There may be circumstances in which it would be good for an ethical actor to state what he or she knew to be untrue. It is obvious that it may well happen that, in precisely the same circumstances, an actor from A and an actor from B will decide correctly, both in accord with their traditions and differently.[32]

This is both obvious and, indeed, commonplace. The present point, however, is that, if the traditions are conceived as logical systems, and if ethical actors are conceived as radically confined within particular systems, and if the different attitudes to stating what is known to be untrue are genuinely postulates, then there is no logical possibility of further argument. The two traditions are simply incommensurable.

Since, by hypothesis, the actors are confined within the logical systems of their respective traditions, there can be no possibility whatsoever of any argument between them.

We must distinguish between discovered differences between traditions and radical relativism. There are, in fact, incompatible ethical traditions. Insofar as ethical actors remain within different incompatible traditions, they will, in fact, sometimes make unarguably incompatible decisions. But it is legitimate to assert a radical relativism only inasmuch as the ethical actors are in principle, and not simply in practice, confined within their mutually incompatible traditions.

The proponents of modern radical relativism more or less clearly recognize this. They all, in their different ways, present ethical actors as fundamentally confined within an already given horizon, or worldview, or episteme, or paradigm, or set of presuppositions, or postulates. In other words, radical relativism assumes that there are logically incompatible systems and that actors are in principle confined within one of them.

It is worth sounding a cautionary note. Not all writers who are impressed, in my view correctly, by the factual relativity of ethical traditions are radical relativists, and not all those who think of themselves as radical relativists are coherently so.

Collingwood, for example, is sometimes taken to be a radical relativist, but he is not. He presented a logic of question and answer, which has been referred to previously, in which propositions were answers to questions; questions emerged from presuppositions; these presuppositions were either relative or absolute; relative presuppositions were themselves answers to earlier questions and so were also propositions; absolute presuppositions were not answers to earlier questions but formed the intellectual context within which questions arose. Intellectual contexts with different and mutually incompatible absolute presuppositions were incommensurable. Inquirers operated within these intellectual contexts. Had Collingwood stopped at that point he would have been a radical relativist. He recognized, however, that an inquirer or a community of inquirers could shift from one set of absolute presuppositions to another, that is, from one basic intellectual context to another.[33]

Recognizing that inquirers and communities of inquirers were not, in principle, confined to the intellectual context or tradition into which they were born, he avoided radical relativism. But he failed, and knew that he had failed, to develop an adequate theory of these momentous intellectual conversions.

Collingwood failed to develop an adequate theory; in fact, he hardly developed a theory of contextual shift at all. But he did clearly repudiate the other possible route to avoiding radical relativism, namely, the assertion that there are postulates that everyone must accept.

That way has been tried for several centuries for both judgments of fact and judgments of value. Underlying the real and important differences between empiricists and rationalists, between modern natural lawyers and command theorists, is the shared concern to discover incontrovertible truths. The empiricist and the rationalist looked for these truths in different places, but they were looking for the same thing and both conspicuously failed to find it. With Peirce, Dewey, Collingwood, Wittgenstein, Heidegger, Sartre, Villey, Sellars, Quine, Lonergan, Kuhn, McIntyre, Rorty, and others I am convinced that these fundamentally incontrovertible given truths simply do not exist. Underlying some real and important—as well as some unreal and petty—differences among modern philosophers from different schools is this common concern: how to account for human knowing and valuing in the full realization that there are no given incontrovertible propositions either of fact or of value.[34]

Collingwood acknowledged that the inquirer was not radically confined within a traditional intellectual context but had no theory to account for it. If radical relativism is not to be the inevitable consequence of the loss of incontrovertible given truths, the repudiation of radical confinement seems the way out of the impasse.

On a historical note, I suspect that both Aristotle and St. Thomas Aquinas were aware, although obscurely, of the importance of this lack of confinement within intellectual horizon or context and that their theory of "first principles," which are not propositions but operations, provides some evidence for the suspicion. That the effort to attain judgments of fact is not confined to a conceptual scheme is suggested by Davidson in his "On the Very Idea of a Conceptual Scheme." The idea of authenticity in Sartre's *Les carnets de la drôle de guerre*, *L'être et le neant*, and elsewhere is an effort to conceive human responsibility as other than confined. In Lonergan's writings with ever-increasing clarity, there is a concern to show how the effort to come to judgments of fact and of value is not confined, in principle, to the traditional intellectual context of the inquirer although it is from within that context, tradition, or horizon that the inquiry begins, and must begin, for that is where the inquirer is.

To escape the confines of logical system, one needs an understanding of human knowing and doing that is not modeled on logical system—an *ethica*, and, indeed, a *scientia, non moro geometrica demonstrata.*

The conclusions of any modern science may be expressed in propositions. These propositions may or may not be coherent with each other; in late nineteenth-century physics, for example, the propositions of electromagnetics were not perfectly consistent with the propositions of mechanics; this strain within physics was one of the factors that led Einstein to relativity mechanics, one of the functions of which was to dispel the conflict between mechanics and the existing electromagnetic theory of Maxwell. The logical analysis of a science has, as one of its functions, the discovery of coherences and incoherences, and the discovery of the latter is a prod to further discovery and invention. The conflict between thesis and antithesis leads to synthesis; in cognitional terms this becomes, The discovered inconsistency between two propositions leads to a demand for resolution. This is the experiential source of coherence theories of truth.

Were there perfect internal consistency within a science at any stage of its development it would be possible to distinguish its propositions into postulates, definitions, and conclusions, and, even where there is not perfect consistency, a provisional and incomplete systematization is possible. Furthermore, there are, in any modern science, elements that are merely supposed and, hence, radically hypothetical. It is the presence of these radically hypothetical elements that led Thomas Kuhn to the discovery of radical revisions. Between pre-Newtonian and Newtonian mechanics there is such a radical revision: before Newton, it was assumed that matter at rest needed no explanation and that what was to be explained was the transition from rest to motion; within Newtonian mechanics, it is assumed that uniform motion requires no explanation and that what requires explanation is divergence from uniform motion, namely, acceleration. Between Newtonian and relativity mechanics there is another radical revision: Newtonian mechanics assumed an absolute space and an absolute time, which formed the framework against which movement was to be measured; relativity mechanics drops the assumption of absolute space and time in favor of a multiplicity of frameworks with transformation equations between them.

Pre-Newtonian mechanics as a *system* is incompatible with Newtonian mechanics as a *system*; Newtonian mechanics as a *system* is incompatible with relativity mechanics as a *system*. The systems as systems are incommensurable and lead to different and incompatible conclusions, as may be illustrated by the commonplace example of the passenger in a moving train who bounces a ball up and down. What is the real trajectory of the ball? In Newtonian mechanics the real trajectory of the ball is the movement of the ball relative to the framework of absolute space; in relativity mechanics there is no single real trajectory of the ball. Relative to the carriage the ball is moving simply up and down. Relative to someone standing at the side of the track and assuming that the earth is stationary, the ball moves in a parabola; relative to the rotation of the earth the ball follows a different course; relative to the rotating earth circling the sun the trajectory is different again—and so on. The prerelativity mechanic asks, What is the *one real*, the *one true*, trajectory? The relativist answer is not that the real trajectory is not known; it is that there is no single real trajectory. The question simply does not arise. As Collingwood puts it, the prerelativist's assumption is simply not made by the relativist.[35]

And, thus, we are faced again with the question, What is the source of ultimate hypothetical elements? If one's understanding of human knowing and valuing is that it is logical system, then one has reached an impasse, for there is no source of these ultimates in the logical system itself. The postulates and axioms in Euclidean geometry cannot be derived within the Euclidean system. I suggest that more ultimate than logical system, more ultimate than the ultimate concepts of any system, is the set of operations that generates all understanding, all knowledge, all systems.

What is ultimate is that set of operations in their operation, not that set of operations as formally known and as expressed in propositions and sentences. If one attempts, whether briefly or at great length, to define this set of operations, then one's definition is a set of propositions that are expressed in sentences. But it is neither these sentences nor the propositions they express that are ultimate; what is ultimate is the set of operations that the propositions attempt to define, refer to, denote.

The point can be illustrated by a discussion of the principle of contradiction. The prime advantage of the example, for present purposes, is that it is not obviously ethical. It has a second advantage in that the phrase used by Aristotle and, following him, Aquinas, to talk of the principle of contradiction is well known. Aristotle said that the principle of contradiction is an instance of a "naturally known first principle." Aquinas concurred. It would seem, that, in the principle of contradiction, we have what, for Aristotle and Aquinas, was an undeniable proposition. Two questions arise. One is interpretive: did Aristotle and Aquinas consider that, when they wrote of the principle of contradiction as naturally known, they were writing of a proposition with which everyone naturally concurred? The second question is theoretical: is the principle of contradiction a naturally known proposition?

I have claimed previously that there are no naturally known propositions, and I do not make an exception for the principle of contradiction. I shall try to show why.

I understand Aristotle and Aquinas to mean that the principle of contradiction is naturally known but not as a proposition is known. This understanding of Aristotle and Aquinas is, I think, plausible, but I shall not argue this interpretive case here.[36]

There follows a short list of ways in which the principle of contradiction may be expressed:

Nothing can both be and not be at the same time and in the same respect.

We cannot assert that something both is and is not at the same time and in the same respect.

$-(p\ \&\ -p)$

$-(p\ \cdot\ -p)$

$NKpNp$

$DpNp$

It is usually not too misleading to say, as I have, that these five sentences each express the principle of contradiction. It is, however, more accurate and, for the present discussion, importantly more accurate, to say that the sentences express the proposition that expresses the concept of the principle of contradiction. The concept arises from the logician's effort to understand an intelligent practice, to conceive that understanding, and to express the concept in a proposition that, in turn, may be expressed in a variety of sentences.

Putting to one side for the moment the first and second sentences, it will be agreed that the four remaining sentences are not identical. All four may be read off as, Not (both) p and not-p. The difference between the third and the fourth sentences is simply that in the third the "&" is used where in the fourth the "." is found. Both are in a version of Peano-Russell notation. The fifth and sixth sentences are in Łukasiewicz or Polish notation.

It must be obvious that the sentences are not "naturally known" since, in order to understand them, one must learn the respective notations and none would claim that either notation is naturally known.

The same, of course, is true of the English sentences. Again, no one suggests that English, or any other natural language, is naturally known.

Accordingly, it is not the sentences, in which the conception of the principle of contradiction is expressed, that are naturally known.

Perhaps it is the proposition, common to the sentences, that is naturally known. This is a more plausible suggestion and it is how the natural knowledge of first principles is often understood. The claim then becomes that we naturally know the proposition or the concept but have to learn the expressions. There are some drawbacks to this approach related to the relation between thought and language, but these are associated with theories of that relation that are many and discordant. There are, however, other drawbacks. Anyone who has taught logic knows that students do not, without instruction, know the answer to either of the following questions:

What is the principle of contradiction?

or

What are the principles of knowing?

and yet, if they knew the principle of contradiction, they would be able to answer the first question fully and correctly and the second question in part. It is, therefore, implausible, on empirical grounds, to claim that humans know the principle of contradiction in any ordinary sense of "know."

On the other hand, if you utter the following, or anything like the following, sentence, you will usually meet resistance:

Ireland is an island and Ireland is not an island.

In order to make sense of what you have said the listener will try a number of strategies and may translate the sentence into:

Ireland is, in some sense, an island and, in some other sense, not an island.

Why will the listener do something like this? The answer is not that the listener knows the principle of contradiction and applies it; it is that the listener is the principle of contradiction and, so, naturally knows that the proposition apparently expressed in your sentence cannot be true. I say "apparently expressed" because, of course, the original sentence may quite easily be a rhetorical way of expressing the perfectly acceptable proposition that, in some sense, Ireland is an island and, in some other sense, it is not. What the listener will not accept is the contradictory proposition because, to use a modern metaphor, listeners are programmed to reject a contradiction once the contradiction is apparent to them.

The *concept* of the principle of contradiction results from the efforts of theorists of knowledge to understand the practice of knowing. The efforts of theorists to understand knowing are not necessarily rewarded with success. Accordingly, some theorists may fail to advert to the principle; some may, more robustly, deny it. As

Aquinas put it, there are two kinds of knowing about knowing. The first, what Aquinas calls "knowledge by presence," is simply the practice of knowing. The second is what he calls "knowledge through causes," and what we might call formal knowledge; this knowledge he thinks is hard to come by; in the effort to gain it, many err (Summa Theologiae I q.87, a.1).

The principle of contradiction is not the object of the person's knowing; it is an element in the person's knowing; it is the fact that the person tends to coherence and consistency. A principle is a source from which something flows; from the principle of contradiction flows coherence. The activity that reveals the principle is the tendency toward coherence.

Theorists may discover the principle of contradiction, and they do so by first making the practice of knowing the object of their inquiry. They may ask what human knowing is and propound the answer that it is an activity in part characterized by the tendency toward coherence. They have called this the principle of contradiction and have formulated their concept of this feature of human knowing in a variety of ways, some of which have been given previously.[37]

Once the principle of contradiction has been discovered and the proposition expressed in a sentence, the proposition can become an axiom in a deductive system. Within the deductive system of which it is an axiom, the principle cannot itself be deduced. Within the system it is basic, neither derived nor derivable, *per se nota*.

The principle of contradiction is, then, "known" in two quite distinct ways. It is "known" in the practice of knowing. In this way it is not the object of knowledge. But it may also be known as an object of knowledge, as what the inquirer is attending to. Indeed, one of the meanings of the phrase *per se nota* ("known by itself") is that the principle of contradiction is not derived: for "something can be said to be known by itself because nothing else is used in coming to know it" (I q.87, a.1, ad 1). To come to the knowledge of conclusions, on the other hand, we do use other things, namely, premises. Accordingly, for Aristotle, conclusions are demonstrable; first principles are not.

Aristotle did write of knowing first principles. He was, I think aware, but perhaps only obscurely, of the two ways of knowing them. That Aquinas distinguishes between these two ways is abundantly clear, but his distinction is difficult to grasp, in part because of the use of the term "knowing." I have distinguished the two ways clearly and, in doing so, have intimated, by putting quotation marks around it, that the term "know" is misleading the first way. I have used it only because it comes down in the tradition, but it may be wiser to drop it entirely.

We may write, instead, of ourselves as coherently present to ourselves in the activity of knowing.

By that coherent presence to self is meant no more than the conscious experiential fact that, when faced with what we know to be a contradiction, we repudiate it. We spontaneously reject the proposition "Ireland is both an island and not an island." That spontaneous rejection is ourselves intelligently and rationally at work. That is why I wrote that we *are* the principle of contradiction.[38]

It should now be clearer what is meant by the claim that what is ultimate is a set of operations in their operation and not a set of operations as known and as expressed in sentences. What is ultimate are operations, not propositions. The principle of contradiction is an operation through which we attain coherence; it is ourselves intellectually and rationally operating coherently. It is that operation that is ultimate. The sentence that expresses the proposition, that expresses the concept of the principle of contradiction, as the object of knowledge, is not ultimate.

The question that we are attempting to address is how we shift from one context to another. It is completely accepted that the contexts as systems may be incompatible and that there is no means of deriving the second context from the first. There must be introduced new postulates. If the only intelligent and rational means of moving from one context to another is by deriving the second from the first, then it follows that, since, by hypothesis, this cannot be done, any contextual shift must be unintelligent and irrational. The general answer to this dilemma is to deny that an intelligent and rational shift from one context to another must be logical. The first step toward that answer is taken by the claim that the ultimates are not the postulates of the systems but the practices of the inquirers.

The source, then, of a shift from one system to another is the inquiring subject who is the set of ultimate operations, that is, the inquiring subject who experiences, who asks about what is experienced, who understands what is experienced, who asks whether the understanding is correct, who judges that it is or that it is not, who asks what is to be done, who suggests possible courses of action, who wonders whether the suggested courses of action are truly worthwhile and who decides to realize one of them.

If inquiring subjects shift from one context to another, and if we are dissatisfied with the idea that such shifts are random, unintelligent, and irrational, we must ask why they do so. The generic answer is quite simple: one is inclined to shift from one context to another because questions have occurred within one's present context that cannot be answered within it. The questions are present. The solutions not only are not present; they are known not to be available within the context. A nice example is provided by the enlargement of sets of numbers in elementary mathematics.

Suppose a student knows the four basic operations of arithmetic ($+$, $-$, $\times$, $\div$) and knows only the set of numbers 1, 2, 3, 4, 5,..., and so on. That student can learn that if any number in the set is added to any number in the set, the result will be another number in the set; for example, $3 + 5 = 8$. The student can go on to learn that the same is true of the operation of multiplication, $\times$. However, if the student plays around with subtraction or division ($-$, $\div$) it will soon dawn that this is not always true; for example, $5 - 4 = 1$ but $5 - 5 = ?$ and $4 - 5 = ?$. There is no number in the set 1, 2, 3, 4, 5,..., that is the answer to the question $5 - 5 = ?$. A question has arisen within the set for which there is no answer within the set. It is not simply that the answer has not been found; it is that there *is* no answer and that it is known that there is no answer. The student may, then, come across another set of numbers, say 0, 1, 2, 3, 4, 5, and now it will be discovered that there is an answer to $5 - 5 = ?$, namely, zero or 0, but that there is still no answer to $4 - 5 = ?$ The context may once again be enlarged to include the negative numbers: -4, -3, -2, -1, 0, 1, 2, 3, 4, and so on. Of course, what the modern student comes across and can easily learn is, once more, the fruit of the immense intellectual effort of others. The student grows intelligently into the tradition.

The point of this simple example is to indicate how questions that arise within the more restricted context can be answered only within the less restricted context.

As long as the student can answer the questions that actually occur there will be no reason to shift from the more to the less restricted context. If we shift now from the student learning a mathematics that is already known to a mathematician moving beyond what is known, we see the same pattern at work. The inventive mathematician will invent because a question has arisen that cannot be answered within the present context.

Of course, not all mathematical invention involves contextual shift. Much mathematics is the exploration of the present context (this corresponds to Kuhn's idea of normal science), but some mathematics does demand contextual shift (and this corresponds to Kuhn's revolutionary science).

Mathematical invention may seem at first sight a far cry from ethics but it is not. The ethical actor is brought up and lives within a tradition. At any moment the ethical actor is his or her tradition. Because tradition is often thought of as simply something outside us, we must remind the reader that one's concrete tradition is oneself situated in the world. One may question one's tradition; that is, one may ask about the adequacy of one's present context. One may agree or disagree. But what is ultimate in action is not the set or collection of more rather than less ultimate propositions; what is ultimate is the spontaneous and unavoidable orientation toward responsible action.

Just as we are the principle of contradiction, so we are this spontaneous and unavoidable orientation toward responsible action.

We find ourselves in a world where the future is, to some extent, to be realized, by and in, actions for which we are responsible.

That assertion calls for some consideration: the future is, to some extent, to be realized, by and in, actions for which we are responsible. As it stands, this is a proposition about the world. It is either true or false.

But where does it stand in this study? I have claimed that no propositions are simply given, and I do not here renege on that claim. Like any other proposition this one must be justified. We may come back to it later; now the focus of attention is on principles that are not propositions but operations.

We are an unavoidable orientation towards action. The basic ethical experience is not a proposition, nor knowing a proposition, but the conscious, intelligent, reasonable, responsible, and totally commonplace experience of asking what one is to do now and whether or not it would be worth doing this or that.

Now, if I ask what I am now to do, I am present to myself as a possibility that may be realized in a number of different ways. The claim being made here is not that I *know* that I am a possibility that may be realized in a number of different ways; nor yet that I am thinking of myself as a possibility, and so forth; nor again that I am the object of an inquiry as to whether or not I am a possibility, et cetera. The claim is that I, as a matter of fact, consciously and responsibly, am that possibility. When I ask what I am to do, I make myself a conscious possibility oriented responsibly toward the future.

The question as to what I am to do looks toward an answer: I am to do X, and to a decision to do it. The future is the possibility of that, as yet unknown, decision, and the field of the possibility of the realization of that decision. The world in which the future is, in part, a possibility to be realized in and by our decisions is, first of all, a necessary context of the question as to what is to be done.

Whether the real world corresponds to this intentional world is a further question. I think the more reasonable position is to claim that it does, but, whatever one's answer, it is crucial to distinguish, in analysis, the real from the intentional world.

Aristotle wrote that we do not deliberate and choose about those things that cannot be otherwise. He was not then considering the question with which we have just been dealing, but, if one supposes that absolutely nothing can be otherwise, then there would be no matter about which to deliberate and choose; there would be neither deliberation nor choice; the question, What am I to do? would simply not arise. Sartre's orientation toward a future for which we are in part responsible, Aristotle's deliberation and choice about those things that can be otherwise, and Lonergan's intention of values are closely allied. For all three, at different times, from different perspectives, are trying to articulate the ethical experience, which is that fundamental, spontaneous, and inescapable orientation toward action that realizes itself from the simple, commonplace, and frequently asked question, What am I to do in this situation?

Aristotle's discussion brings one further clarification, which should be noted briefly. Not everyone will agree about what can and cannot be otherwise, so, when one thinks of the ethical actor asking what is to be done in this situation, what is meant by "this situation" is, of course, this situation as it appears to him or her. So, some years ago, most people in modern Western civilization thought that, for the most part, nothing could be done about the climate. For them the climate was, accordingly, not something about which they deliberated. Now, however, when, for example, more people are becoming convinced that even the use of aerosol sprays crucially affects the world's climate, even if not in the short term, the climate does become a matter of deliberation and choice.[39] In other words, purely factual knowledge or technical expertise does enter into the ethical field by shifting something from the realm of that about which nothing can be done (what, very roughly, Aristotle called "the necessary") into the realm of those things that can be otherwise, the realm of the possible. Most people do not consider that the past can be changed and so do not deliberate about it; were someone to think otherwise, he could deliberate about it. And, more importantly, were someone to deliberate about the past, he would be committed to taking the past as changeable. Not only do we not, as a matter of fact, deliberate about that which we know not to be changeable; we *cannot* do so, any more than we can affirm a proposition that we know to be contradictory. To engage in deliberation and choice engages us in an operative interpretation of the world. Ethical action has ontological consequences, although we do not know these when we are acting. These consequences are discovered with difficulty by the theorist who may err.

The basic ethical operations of asking what I must do, considering the situation; working out possible courses of action; determining which of these are practicable; wondering which are truly valuable, really better, more worthwhile; and eventually deciding, constitute the first principle of ethics. The ethical subject is the one who asks, wonders, determines, reflects, and decides. The ethical subject is, then, the first principle of ethical action.[40]

Just as the principle of contradiction is the knowing subject's acting coherently, so the traditional ethical principle that the good must be done is the ethical subject's asking, wondering, determining, and deciding.[41] Just as the principle of contradiction can become the object of knowledge, and an understanding of it expressed in the sentence NKpNp, so the ethical principle can become the object of knowledge and an understanding of it expressed in the sentence "The good is to be done." As the principle of contradiction so expressed can be used as a premise in an argument or as an axiom in a system, so the proposition that the good is to be done can be used in a practical syllogism.

And so we return at last to the question of the criterion: How am I to know if a course of action is truly good, truly worthwhile, really better, more valuable than another?

Just as there is a naive correspondence theory of truth that holds that one can, in judging, attain a position above both proposition and reality and compare the two, so there is a naive correspondence theory of the ethical criterion that holds that in judging whether something is good, one attains a higher position and can compare the proposed course of action against, for example, a rule or an innate law.

Many modern attacks on the correspondence theory of truth are attacks against this version of it. This is not too unreasonable since this version is, doubtless, the dominant one. The attacks are well founded, but they err in assuming that correspondence theory is confined to such naïveté.

Rorty remarks that many philosophical theories are images in another guise.[42] Quintillian, before him, noticed that almost everything we say is metaphor. In the naive version of correspondence theory there lurks a beguiling image. The image has several variants, but one of the most immediately appealing is the activity of comparing a pictorial representation, drawing, painting, or photograph with its subject, in order to discover whether the representation looks like the original. In this case, one already has an image of the original and one is asked whether the second image is like the first. One can, as it were, stand back from both and compare them. Next one supposes that one of the images is the criterion against which the other is to be judged. Perhaps in most everyday situations, the criterion is one's image of, for example, the real person against whom we compare the photograph but the reverse is not unusual. The passport controller uses the photograph as the criterion against which to judge the identity of the real person claiming to be the person represented. Still, whatever image is taken to be the criterion, both images are equally available. Naive correspondence theory is a more or less sophisticated, more or less concealed, application of such an image.

In order to extirpate naive correspondence theory completely it is necessary to show that it is not an adequate account even of the activity that superficially seems to confirm it. I shall try to show, therefore, that

naive correspondence theory is not an adequate account
of how we compare a photograph of a person with that
person. The passport controller's question is this: Is this
person standing before me the person whose photograph
is in the passport? The controller has two relevant
images: the image of the real person on the one hand,
the image of the photograph on the other. The first
image is obtained by looking at the person; the second,
by looking at the photograph. We may take it that the
controller is expert in the interpretation of this kind of
photograph. Let us suppose that, in a particular case,
the controller discerns a similarity between the two
images. The controller has not yet answered the question. The operative question now becomes, Is the perceived similarity sufficient evidence for the judgment
that the person presenting the passport is the person
represented in the passport photograph? The controller
has two pieces of evidence: the image of the real person
and the photographic image. And neither image can be
the criterion for the judgment, for the images are simply
images. The perceived similarity, which is neither image,
occurs within the controller, who must ask whether it
is sufficient evidence for the judgment; the perceived
similarity is, then, a third piece of data distinct from
both original images. Still, the perceived similarity is
not the criterion, for the controller must ask whether
it is sufficient evidence for the judgment that the person
represented in the photograph is the same person as
the one who is now presenting the passport. The criterion for that judgment is the grasp of the sufficiency
of that evidence.

In this brief analysis, I have written of "perceived
similarity" as if this were obvious and uncontroversial.
It is not. To perceive a visual similarity between, say,
one penny and another penny is very different from
perceiving a similarity between a photograph and its
original. In our culture, we learn how to interpret pho-

tographs and other visual images, so that our perception of similarities is rapid and habitual. The passport controller's expertise is a further development and specialization of this culturally learned skill. (Anyone who doubts that this is a culturally learned skill should try to recognize similarities between one Chinese ideograph and another!) In some cases, we do not "at once" perceive the similarity between photograph and original and must work our way bit by bit to a hypothesis of similarity. A commonplace example is the difficulty we often experience when trying to discover, in a photograph of a group of young children, which one of them has become a particular adult.

Naive correspondence theory is not yet fully undermined. There are other examples, some of them more immediately moral. Quite often candidates are admitted to programs if and only if they fulfill certain conditions. Leaving aside difficult cases—and there always will be difficult cases in practice—let us ask how apparently simple cases are to be understood.

Suppose that a sufficient and necessary entry condition to a degree program were a B in mathematics in the entrance examination. Do we not then simply compare the candidate's results with the condition? The answer is, I think, that this is, indeed, what we do. In fact, we commonly do so algorithmically in a suitably designed computer program the logical structure of which is

Entry iff B in maths in the examination
(Insert examination result)
(Enter if B; reject if − B)

But this logical structure serves only to show that we are back again with a fundamental premise—in this example, "Enter iff B in the examination"—that simply cannot be justified within the system. Thus, naive correspondence theory in the moral or ethical domain requires a set of in the end unjustifiable fundamental propositions or injunctions.

Because the attacks against correspondence theory are in fact attacks against the image of comparing one thing (the judgment) with something else (reality), they are successful but also lead to an inability to account adequately for judgment. Another version of correspondence theory is both necessary and possible.

Consider the proposition "Atahuallpa was the last emperor of the Incas." This proposition is true if and only if Atahuallpa was the last emperor of the Incas.

Distinguish between a proposition's being known to be true and a proposition's being true. If we suppose that a proposition is either true or false, then we do not need to know whether or not a given proposition is true before we can confidently assert that it is true if and only if the state of affairs that it asserts to be the case is in fact the case. I can confidently claim that the proposition "Atahuallpa was the last emperor of the Incas" is true if and only if Atahuallpa was the last emperor of the Incas, even if no one *knows* whether or not he was. This is so of any proposition whatsoever. So the proposition "Pegasus is a flying horse" is true if and only if Pegasus is a flying horse. This is no more than an application of Tarski.

The claim "Pegasus is a flying horse" can be both true and false—true if what is meant is that Pegasus is a character in a myth and false if what is meant is that Pegasus is a real horse that can fly—is easily met by distinguishing between sentences and propositions. Sentences may be ambiguous; propositions are not. So the sentence "Pegasus is a flying horse" may express the proposition that there was a character in a myth that was a flying horse and was called Pegasus or the proposition that there was a real horse whose name was Pegasus and that could fly. These are quite distinct propositions and have quite distinct, independent, and

unrelated truth conditions. There is no theoretical problem whatsoever in claiming that one is true and the
other false.

It may be difficult in some cases to determine which
proposition the sentence expresses, but, in all cases, it
is the proposition, not the sentence, that is either true
of false. Properly speaking, sentences are neither true
nor false but adequate or inadequate expressions of the
propositions that they express.

Once the distinction between a proposition's being
true or false and being known to be true or false is
made clear, it becomes possible to clarify some obscu-
rities. It may be difficult or even impossible for us to
know whether or not Atahuallpa was the last emperor
of the Incas, but, as far as I can discover, nobody wants
to hold any of the following:

(i) Atahuallpa was the last emperor of the Incas, but the
proposition "Atahuallpa was the last emperor of the Incas"
is false.

(ii) Atahuallpa was not the last emperor of the Incas, but
the proposition "Atahuallpa was the last emperor of the
Incas" is true.

(iii) Atahuallpa was the last emperor of the Incas, but the
proposition "Atahuallpa was the last emperor of the Incas"
is neither true nor false.

(iv) Atahuallpa was not the last emperor of the Incas, but
the proposition "Atahuallpa was the last emperor of the
Incas" is neither true nor false.

Again, as far as I can discover, nobody genuinely wants
to hold the following (though some writers fudge the
issue):

(v) Atahuallpa both was and was not the last emperor of
the Incas.

The remark about propositions (i), (ii), (iii), and (iv) is an application of Tarski's principle that the proposition *p* is true, if and only if the state of affairs *p* obtains.

If one wants to hold that proposition (v) is true, one is committed to repudiating the principle of contradiction, and this one cannot do in practice. Unless sentence (v) is interpreted to express simultaneously (ambiguously) two noncontradictory propositions, it expresses a contradiction and is, strictly, meaningless.

When the distinction between a proposition's being true or false and being known to be true or false is made, it is possible to distinguish between those who hold that something is the case but that this cannot be known and those who hold that nothing is the case. Since few, if any, hold that nothing is the case (proposition [v]), we can move to the question as to how one knows that a proposition is true or false.

The naive correspondence theory, successfully attacked by many modern writers, asserts that one can compare the proposition with the reality. This cannot be done and, were it possible, it would be redundant.

A proposition is true if and only if the state of affairs that it asserts obtains. A proposition is known to be true if the judging subject has sufficient evidence to come to the judgment, Such and such is the case.

Accordingly, for me to know that Atahuallpa was the last emperor of the Incas requires that I (not somebody else, but I) have sufficient evidence. For whom is the evidence sufficient? And what does "sufficient" mean? If I am really asking whether I know and not whether someone else or people in general know, then the evidence must be sufficient for me. It is not enough that it be sufficient for someone else; if I am to know something, then the evidence must be sufficient for me. And sufficient for me means that I have no further questions, that I am, as a matter of fact, convinced. That someone else is convinced is a matter of indifference except insofar as the other being convinced is a reason for my believing the proposition or a reason for me to continue my investigation. If it is I who wants to know, then it is I who must be convinced.

When I grasp that the evidence is sufficient and judge that something is the case, then I claim that it is the case independent of my judging. That is, I claim that the fact that I am convinced is not part of the evidence for the thing's being the case.

This position has some consequences. It may be that I am too easily convinced or that I am obstinate; that I am too ignorant to grasp that something constitutes evidence; that the evidence does not yet exist (for example, a medical diagnosis often requires the development of the illness—from the epistemological point of view, the production of further evidence—before the diagnostician will affirm a tentative proposition); that the necessary evidence is lost (for example, a document known to have existed and known to have been destroyed may condemn a historical suggestion to remain forever conjecture). Most fundamentally, the criterion of the true judgment of fact is not a reality that may be compared with the proposition; it is rather the inquiring and reasonable subject.

What of the judgment of value? I ask what I am to do now and propose a course of action. I ask whether the proposed course of action is good, better, more important, more urgent than another. I examine the proposal in the light of my situation and seek reasons for and against the suggestion; I allow time for questions to arise, for advantages and difficulties to occur to me. But in the end I am convinced: once again, it is I, not someone else, who is convinced. Although I may well have used rules in the process of coming to my judgment and decision, the criterion is not a rule but the fact that I am convinced. Generalizing, the criterion is the responsible subject: what Aristotle called the prudent man and Sartre the authentic person and what, in the medieval tradition, was called a quiet conscience. The actual criterion of ethical action is the ethical subject.

As there was a distinction between knowing that a proposition of fact was true and its being true, so there is a distinction between knowing a judgment or prop-osition of value to be true and its being true. The judgment or proposition of value asserts that a proposed course of action is, say, the most valuable in the present circumstances. This proposition is true if and only if the proposed course of action is the most valuable in the present circumstances. It is, obviously, an extremely relevant question as to how one knows that a proposed course of action is or is not the most valuable in the circumstances, but it is also a different question.

The proper objection at this juncture is that the proposition that "Proposed course of action X is the most valuable course of action in the circumstances" cannot be true because there is no such thing as the most valuable course of action in the circumstances. Note that the objection is not that the most valuable course of action cannot be known (this can be another and later objection); it is quite simply that there is no such thing as the most valuable course of action in the circumstances.

The objection may be understood in several ways. It may mean that in all circumstances there are several courses of action that are equally valuable as well as a far greater number of less valuable courses of action. It may mean that in some circumstances, including this one, there are several equally valuable courses of action as well as a far greater number of less valuable possible courses of action. Or it may mean that all possible courses of action are always equally valuable (or valueless).

Now, it does not seem plausible to claim that in all possible circumstances, all possible courses of action are equally valuable (or valueless). If, for example, one wants to know the meaning in English of the Norwegian neuter noun *vann*, it is more valuable to look in a Norwegian-English than in a French-English dictionary.

As for the objection that in all circumstances several possible courses of action are equally valuable, it is wise to distinguish. It seems likely enough that in some, perhaps most, circumstances there are several equally valuable possibilities. But it does not seem very difficult to imagine circumstances in which one of the possible courses of action is more valuable than any other. If one were in extreme need of liquid it might be that to drink either of two available liquids would be equally valuable, but if only one potable liquid were available, the most valuable course of action would be to drink it.

These examples are, of course, deliberately simple because the present issue is not that it is always easy to discover what the best course of action is, but simply to show that there are relatively more and less valuable possible courses of action. This clears the way to an account of how these may be discovered.

There remains a relevant objection against the examples and the interpretation of them, namely, that the valued action in both cases is valued only because it is a means to the realization of a prior value. Clearly, however, this objection does not indicate that no course of action is better than another but simply that courses of action are valuable or worthless, more or less worthwhile, more or less urgent, within situations in part defined by the context of the actor.

This clarification of the objection itself clarifies the precise distinction between judgments of fact and judgments of value. If something is the case, then it is the case, whether or not anyone knows it and whether or not anyone is interested. If one makes the judgment that something is the case, then the fact that one makes the judgment is not part of the evidence for the truth of the judgment. If one makes the judgment that something is the case, then the judgment is true if and only if what is judged to be so is so. The truth of the judgment is not independent of the judgment since it is a property of the judgment, but the fact that something is the case is independent of the judgment.

On the other hand, if something is valuable, then it is valuable in relation to a valuer. If I claim that studying philosophy is valuable, I must mean that it is valuable for someone—I have not yet specified for whom—to study philosophy. If it is the case that studying philosophy is valuable for no one, then studying philosophy is not valuable and the claim that it is is mistaken. I can go on to make the claim that to study philosophy would be valuable for students of economics even though no student of economics yet knows this. In more general terms, I can make the claim that a certain course of action is, or would be, valuable for people within a given context and a given situation, even if no one within that context and situation knew it. There are considerable problems about this claim that have yet to be faced, but even if it is allowed for the moment, some of its consequences need articulation.

Even if there is, in some sense, a truly valuable course of action in the circumstances, it is still the case that this must be discovered by the actor and the actor must be convinced that a proposed course of action is truly valuable. But for the actor to be convinced, sufficient evidence must be produced and, once again, the evidence must be sufficient for the actor concerned. If I am the actor concerned, the evidence must be sufficient for me. If you are, then it must be sufficient for you. Of course, it is possible that the same evidence would be sufficient for both of us—indeed, one of the features of a scientific community is that the members agree about what constitutes sufficient evidence and one of the things that the neophyte learns is what constitutes evidence in the tradition—but it is equally possible that the same evidence would not be sufficient for both of us.

In the ethical field will the same evidence be sufficient for everyone? The ambiguity behind this question is by now sufficiently well known to need no further elaboration, but this much is clear: subjects differ from one another in their traditions, in their emotional, intellectual, social, cultural, aesthetic, moral, and spiritual development, and so it is most unlikely that what constitutes sufficient evidence for one person will always be sufficient evidence for another very different person.

Consequent is that people will as a matter of fact differ in their evaluations. The theory predicts this difference. And since this difference in fact occurs and people do, as a matter of fact, differ in their evaluations, it would be strange to put forward a theory of ethical action that did not predict, and was unable to account for, this divergence.

The theory does not require that different people differ in their evaluations of everything. Once again, as a matter of fact, just as there is ethical divergence, there is also ethical agreement, and a theory of ethical action must be able to account for this. The general answer is that if people share a tradition, they share a set of evaluations and this shared background is likely to lead to considerable agreement in new evaluations.

One can be mistaken in one's judgment of value, although, at the moment of making this or any other kind of mistake, one cannot know that one is mistaken. One may, for example, overlook a feature of the situation that one would have taken into account had it been pointed out. One may give less weight to something than, in retrospect, one recognizes should have been given. It is not difficult to discern obtuseness in others if not in ourselves. Nor is it uncommon to come across people with a delicate and nuanced feel for the niceties of different situations.

One may make a mistake in a judgment of value because one has made a prior mistake in a judgment of fact. Thus, if someone judges that she should have an abortion and grounds this judgment in part on the judgment of fact that the human fetus is not a human person, then, if the judgment of fact is mistaken, so too may be the judgment of value. The logic of this requires clarification. Suppose a person argues thus:

> If the human fetus is not a human person, then I should have an abortion.
> The human fetus is not a human person.
> Consequently, I should have an abortion.

This argument is valid. Accordingly, if both premises are true the conclusion is true. But what if the second premise is false? It does not follow that the conclusion is false. Nor, consequently, does it follow that the negation of the conclusion "I should not have an abortion" is true. What follows is that the person now has no argument for her conclusion and that her conclusion—as far as the argument is concerned—may be true or false.

However, the person's position and argument may be crucially different. Her argument may be:

> If and only if the human fetus is not a human person, then I should have an abortion.
> The human fetus is not a human person.
> Consequently, I should have an abortion.

In this case, if the second premise is false the negative conclusion, that she should not have an abortion, follows. The mistaken judgment of fact leads to a mistaken conclusion, but, of course, only within the ethical context defined here by the major premise.

This suggests yet another way in which one's judgment of value may be mistaken. One may be mistaken because one's ethical horizon or context is restricted. Thus, a selfish person will judge valuable what a more selfless person would judge valueless, less valuable, less important, and so on.

The suggestion that people can be mistaken because their ethical horizons are restricted is highly controversial and must be dealt with at greater length.

Some consequences of the suggestion should be admitted at once. It involves me in the assertion that some people are better than others within a tradition and, perhaps, that some traditions are better—that is, less restricted—than others. However, the suggestion does not involve me in the assertion that if two traditions are different, or if two people within the one tradition are different, one in necessarily better than the other.

This is a fairly unfashionable position. The more fashionable positions are either that there is one best horizon or that there is an indefinite number of incommensurable and equally good horizons. Notice that a radical theory of incommensurable and equally good horizons excludes an account of ethical development; it allows for horizon shift but not for development or decline.

If one horizon is better than another, and if this can be known, then there must be some criterion to enable one to discriminate. In the history of Western ethical theory that criterion has been thought to be a principle or set of principles conceived as propositions. The suggestion advanced here is that the grounding principle or criterion is not a sentence nor a proposition but a subject: the questioning ethical subject who asks what should now be done. This subject may move from horizon to horizon, by raising questions in the more restricted horizon, that are not answerable within it and so constructing a new horizon within which they are answerable. And this new horizon is itself provisional since questions may arise within it that are not answerable within it, thus giving rise to the construction of yet another horizon, and so on.

Of this idea of developing horizons two things may be said. First, the set of operations that the subject is is not confined within any of these provisional horizons. Were the subject confined within any provisional horizon, then movement from one to another would be impossible. Were there no operation moving the subject from one horizon to another, the shift would be, in the end, random and arbitrary. The idea of the question as the operator, not only within horizons but also from horizon to horizon, both accounts for the *fact* of development and grounds its reasonableness. Development is not simply a shift from one horizon to another; it is a shift from a horizon within which questions arise but cannot be answered to a horizon within which those questions can be answered. Development can be personal but it can also be social, inasmuch as the more developed horizon becomes the tradition that the next generation learns.

The set of operations moves the subject and, through the cooperation of individuals, the society and the culture through a sequence of developing horizons. The subject thus intends—in the activity itself and not in a theoretic or reflective by-product of the activity—this development from horizon to horizon. When this spontaneous intention is theoretically understood, a further question arises: Is there any halt to this development from horizon to horizon; is there a final, completely adequate, definitive horizon? A horizon is provisional because questions can arise within it that are not answerable within it: that is, the specification of the good that emerges within it is not beyond criticism. It is, therefore, possible to say what a final, completely adequate, definitive horizon would be. It would be a horizon within which all possible questions could be answered: that is, the specification of the good that arose within it would be beyond criticism, not because it is not permissible to ask questions but because those questions can be satisfactorily answered. We can, therefore, say that the subject in his spontaneous ethical operations intends the good as specified in this horizon, that is, intends the good that is beyond criticism.

Whether and how such a horizon exists, whether the ethical subject can attain it, are important, but later questions. The question as to its existence will not be addressed fully here, but some clarificatory points need to be made.

If it is the case, as I have claimed, that the final completely adequate horizon within which the good beyond criticism may be specified is intended by the ethical subject, then, correlatively, this final horizon is an intentional object.

Ethical subjects move from horizon to horizon. Were an ethical subject so to develop that there was a coincidence between this intentional horizon and the actual horizon, then the final horizon would exist as the horizon of that particular ethical subject.

It is clear that the question of the existence of the final horizon may be analyzed into several distinct questions. First, does the adequate horizon exist as an intentional object? Second, is the adequate horizon coincident with the actual horizon of any ethical subject? Third, does it have any other kind of existence? These questions may, in their turn, be further analyzed. For present purposes it is worth examining the first.

The theory put forward here is that the adequate horizon exists as the intentional goal of every ethical subject. However, it is no part of the theory that every ethical subject has studied ethical action and advances this theory. There is, then, a distinction between the adequate horizon as a spontaneously operative intentional goal in ethical action and the adequate horizon as a feature of a theory of ethical action.

As there can be a development of horizons, so also can there be retraction from a more to a less encompassing horizon within which questions that arose in the former horizon no longer appear. This decline can come about through a refusal to act in accord with the demands within the larger horizon, followed by subsequent rationalization until the good as specified within the larger horizon no longer seems good. This decline can occur within the ethical biography of a single person, but decline, as much as development, can be social, so that the next generation of children are educated within the more restricted horizon that their parents have adopted, rather than within the larger horizon within which their parents were brought up but that they abandoned.

Because of this dual possibility of development or decline there is not merely a history but a dialectic of horizons and once again the question of criterion arises. Whatever horizon one is in, it seems possible to discern that there are different horizons and to compare them dialectically: that is, to discover and contrast the more basic propositions and orientations within the several horizons.

It is less easy to place the horizons in order, since to someone within a more restricted horizon, a more extended horizon may seem not more encompassing but simply mistaken. Plato's *Gorgias* is a dialectic of horizons and within it Callicles is presented as unable to discern the value of Socrates' horizon from the vantage of his own.

And so another consequence of the theory of development and decline must be faced. The person in the more encompassing horizon is in a position to judge correctly the conclusions within the more restricted horizon, but the reverse is not the case. As long as Callicles remains within his restricted horizon it is simply not possible to convince him of Socrates' values. The issue is not that it is difficult to persuade Callicles. It is not difficult but impossible. As long as both remain within their incompatible horizons, they cannot agree and neither can demonstrate his conclusions to the other. The philosopher coming back into the cave, in Plato's story, cannot convince the denizens of darkness until their horizons have been expanded. Plato's dialectic is not a dialectic of propositions but a dialectic of horizons.

For antagonists within different and incompatible horizons there can be no agreement on the basic issues that define their differences. This leads some to the conclusion that there is no "objectivity" but only "subjective" opinion. These terms rarely illumine and frequently obscure beyond recovery, but it is worth seeing how far the present position goes along one line of meaning sometimes attributed to them. That there is no "objectivity" often means that there is no agreed criterion or set of criteria, axioms, or presuppositions that can be used to settle issues. The term rarely means only that, and there is often an unacknowledged penumbra that serves to obfuscate issues. But in that meaning of the term, between antagonists within different and incompatible horizons, there is no "objectivity." The basic judgments are "subjective" insofar as each relies on attitudes that the other rejects. But it is utterly crucial to notice that none of this is incompatible with the idea of one of the antagonists' being correct and the other mistaken; what is the case is simply that, as long as both remain within their incompatible horizons, neither can convince the other.

Suppose that I am convinced that my horizon is more encompassing than my partner's. As long as he remains within this horizon I cannot convince him of this, for to convince him of this is to lead him from his horizon to mine. Furthermore, I cannot, from within his horizon, demonstrate the superiority of mine, because the su-

periority of mine does not follow from premises within
his.

Demonstration is one kind of persuasion, but there
are other kinds and it has been shown that demonstration is not the kind of persuasion apt to the task
of moving one's partner from a less to a more developed
horizon. There is required another rhetoric in practice
and, in ethical theory, a theory of that rhetoric. This
question will be taken up later; meanwhile, I want to
turn to a comparative inquiry.

In his well-known *The Idea of a Social Science* and in
"Understanding a Primitive Society" Peter Winch analyzed E. E. Evans-Pritchard's study of Zande witchcraft,
oracles, and magic in an effort to illustrate one interpretation and a possible application of Wittgenstein's
theory of language games.[43] According to Winch, the
Azande and we were simply acting within two different
worlds so that what to them seemed rational to us
seemed irrational. The importance of Winch's study,
and one of the important contributions made by Evans-
Pritchard's work, was to show clearly that everyday
reasonable behavior was contextual. People did X because they assumed Y to be the case, but people differed
in their contexts and so produced different responses.
This is now so thoroughly accepted that it is sometimes
difficult to appreciate quite how much fieldwork,
thought, and writing went into the effort to persuade
us of it. My interest in Zande practices is not simply
one more effort to do what has been quite adequately
done already but to rediscover a common practice beneath by now well-known differences.

I shall give two examples of Zande practice. First, the
Azande believed that unpleasant chance occurrences
were due to the evil influences of their enemies who
were "witches." "Witches" and "witchcraft" are the accepted translations of the Zande terms, but Zande
witches are not witches in the European sense. They

are people with a congenital capacity to effect ill upon their enemies, not by deciding to do so but simply by thinking evilly of them.

If a man were walking under his barn and the barn fell upon him, causing him some injury, he would attribute this to witchcraft. He would know very well that the barn fell because the supporting beams had been eaten through by termites. What witchcraft explains is why the barn fell at exactly the time he was walking under it. What witchcraft explains is what we call chance or coincidence and, more specifically, unwelcome chance or coincidence.

This may be taken as an example of what we would tend to call irrational. It is not an irrational interpretation for Azande, and we have no difficulty in understanding that it is not an irrational interpretation or explanation, once we know of the basic idea that unpleasant coincidence is due to witchcraft. That basic idea may be irrational—is it irrational or mistaken?—but that is not the present point.

Not only would it not be irrational for a Zande to think that he had been bewitched; it would be irrational for him to fail to explain the event thus. In just the same way, it may or may not be irrational to attribute every event to an omnipotent and omniscient Providence, but, if one does so understand every event, then it is irrational not to attribute a given particular event to Providence.

So much is obvious. Slightly less obvious is the observation that the Zande question as to how to account for unpleasant coincidence is a question that occurs to us too. More fundamentally still, it is a question that could occur to us, even if it had not already done so.

The Zande answer differs from our answer—there is not now, in any event, a single culturally accepted answer in Western culture; our answers range from Providence, to astrological accounts of the influence of

the stars, to unexplained and unexplainable chance—
and it is their answer that makes them live in a world
different from ours. By their question they live in the
same world. Since their question is a specification of
questioning, by their questions they reveal themselves
to share the same operations that I have called basic.
By their question as to how to account for coincidence
they reveal that they want to know how to account for
coincidence correctly.

The Zande view is that witchcraft accounts for unwelcome coincidence. That view gives rise to further
questions. Since we do not share the view, these further
questions are not ours because questions, as Collingwood
has shown, arise on presuppositions and we do not
share the relevant presuppositions. The further questions
yield further answers, which give rise to still more questions, and an increasingly elaborate culture is built up,
which is increasingly alien to someone to whom the
initial conditions, so to speak, are alien.

Azande live in a different world from us, play a
different game, but they are fundamentally different
from us only if they are, by nature and in principle,
confined to their answers and we to ours. There are
simply no grounds for asserting this. One of Donald
Davidson's[44] arguments against confinement within conceptual schemes is that, were we so confined, we should
be unable to understand any conceptual scheme other
than our own—which is not the case. Another related
argument is that, were we so confined, we should be
unable to convert from one scheme to another—which,
again, is not the case.

I have referred to the Zande answer. The proposition
that unwelcome coincidence is caused by witchcraft is
very basic in Zande culture, but it is not, in principle,
an unquestionable axiom, for it is, I suggest, an answer
to a question, How are we to account for unwelcome
coincidence? But why should that question arise? Col-

lingwood suggests that questions arise on presuppositions that seem to be like sentences and that, eventually,
one gets back to unquestionable presuppositions. I suggest that questions have two sources: an experiential
source and an intellectual source. The experiential
source is our living in the world; the intellectual source
is the fact that we are beings who ask questions. Everyone by nature wonders and what is wondered about is
experience. So Azande ask about unwelcome coincidence because unwelcome coincidence is an important
feature of their lives and because they are human.[45]

The second example is the practice of dealing with
witchcraft. The Zande injured by the falling barn, thinking that this is due to some enemy's witchcraft, asks;
Who did it? The first response to this question is another
question: Are you sure that this event was a coincidence
in the relevant sense? Thus, Evans-Pritchard writes that
a farmer who complains that his groundnut harvest is
poor relative to his neighbor's may be told that this is
entirely due to his bad farming and that he has no
case. Once it has been established that there has been
a relevant coincidence, then the question of responsiblity
is given full sway and oracles are consulted to discover
the culprit.

The simplest oracle (the oracle of first instance) is the
rubbing board oracle, which is asked to cause the rubbing pestle to stick if *NN* (a named person) is the culprit.
NN is not chosen at random; the injured party casts
about in his mind among those he thinks are his enemies
and chooses first the one he considers most likely (the
one against whom he considers there to be a prima facie
case). If the matter is serious or the rubbing board oracle
has been in some way unsatisfactory—giving, for example, randomly different and conflicting answers—then
there is an appeal to the chicken oracle (the oracle of
second instance or appeal). Beyond this a further appeal

is possible to the supreme oracle, the prince's chicken oracle.

When the culprit has been identified, that is, when the question, Who did it? Who is guilty? has been answered, the properly judicial question arises: What is due? In general, what is due is that the culprit repent, effect some reconciliation with the injured party, and, perhaps, make some redress. It is likewise due that he be given an opportunity to do these things.

I have described Zande procedure in such a way that my comparison with our judicial procedures will appear more clearly, but I doubt that the reader of *Witchcraft, Oracles and Magic among the Azande* would be in the least disconcerted by my presentation.

Since we do not believe in witchcraft, we should find the whole process vitiated from the start. Futhermore, even if we did think a tort had been committed, we should not be inclined to accept the oracles as adequate methods for determining guilt (analogous methods were, of course, used in Europe in earlier times, trial by ordeal, for example). With respect to much of the content, we and the Azande are within different worlds, different horizons, paradigms, perspectives, conceptual schemes, language games, or whatever.

But structurally, what the Azande try to do by their system is what we try to do by our system of courts. In both cases a tort gives rise to the question as to who is liable and, when this has been settled, to the question as to what is due. In both cases, there is a system of appeal from lower to higher adjudication and to an adjudication of final appeal.

A common misunderstanding of our adjudicative process is that courts exist to determine guilt or innocence. They do not. Their proper function is to determine what is due to the several parties in the action. In the course of fulfilling this task, it often happens that the courts must answer the prior question of innocence or guilt, since what is due to someone sometimes depends on his guilt or innocence. The Zande oracles address this prior question. Undoubtedly we should not find them satisfactory, but closer investigation shows how they do answer—however badly—questions that we, just as much as the Azande, ask.

If I think that someone has done me a wrong but am not certain of this, one way of trying to find out is to ask him. The obivous problem is that he may lie. To circumvent this problem, I may try to invent a method of discovering the truth less dependent on what he chooses to tell me. Since this is quite a commonplace problem, we may expect that adjudicative systems will, over the years, have worked out various methods: investigating officials, circumstantial evidence, cross-examinations, witnesses, alibis, and so on. All these techniques are aids to answering the question; Is the accused person guilty? In the end, then, whatever method is adopted must yield the answer yes or no. In the common law system, a well-known method is the jury, which gives one of these answers after its assessment of the arguments made before it. It is part of the system that the jury is normally required to do this. It may not normally refuse to conclude. If it considers the evidence insufficient it must return the verdict "not guilty" (or, in Scotland, either "not proven" or "not guilty").

Among the Azande, too, you could attempt to find out whether someone were bewitching you by asking him. But there, too, the method has the same obvious limitations. There is then the effort to discover a method of answering the relevant question that is not so closely linked to personal interest. The oracle is, like the jury, more or less unbiased. The physical structure of both the rubbing board and the chicken oracle is, for this purpose, the same. Sometimes the pestle sticks and sometimes it does not; sometimes the chicken dies of the poison that is administered to it and sometimes it does not. It is this yes-no structure of the method that is significant; both oracles would be useless if they always did the same thing. This is so obvious that it may blind us to the much more significant discovery that the Azande are trying to deal with, and know they are trying to deal with, the same question as we. It is precisely because they are trying to deal with the same question that we can even begin to make the claim that our answer is better than theirs. But it is also because they have the same question, and the same ability to question their answers, that Zande culture could in principle have moved from oracles to some other technique just as European culture abandoned the trial by ordeal.

The emergence of questions is not confined to the West, and there is an unacknowledged racism, a racism that would be utterly repudiated were it to become clear, in some genuinely well-meaning attempts to preserve cultures. It is true that questions do not arise within the system conceived as a finished product. But, then, questions do not arise within systems. Questions arise within subjects.

Just as the Zande oracles are a technique for getting certain answers, so our adjudicative practices are techniques. These techniques are discoveries and there is a history of such discoveries. I am by no means assuming that our present practices are perfect. Indeed, it is crucial to the position put forward here that these practices are in principle subject to further questions. To ask whether the jury system is a good way of determining guilt or innocence in a criminal trial is legitimate. To ask whether the adversarial system of the common law is better, less good, or merely other than the inquisitorial system of the civil law is legitimate.

When certain facts have been established, then does the question of what is due to whom properly arise. When it has been established that *NN* caused the barn to fall on *AA*, the issue of the future relations between the two properly arises. As we now see things in Western culture generally, the real issue is damages: *NN* must pay damages to *AA*; the court settles the amount due and the matter is thus settled.

The Azande answer the same question somewhat differently. For them damages are not the really crucial issue. For them reconciliation seems to be more crucial. The real issue is the enmity between the parties, and it is this that, as far as possible, must be overcome. What is due is that the disputants must participate in a reconciliation ritual in which the offender repudiates his offense and the offended party accepts the repentance.

In this answer to the question of what is due, the Azande show an understanding of a very significant aspect of human affairs. The proverb has it that what is done cannot be undone. This is true but there is more to be said. For people can regret what has been done. It is sometimes said that it is no use being sorry; in fact it is, often, no use being anything else, for the deed cannot be undone and repair is possible only if the injured person accepts the gesture. We concentrate on what is due to the injured party, namely damages from the offender, to the almost complete overlooking of what may be due from the injured party to the offender, namely, forgiveness. It is this fuller vision of what is due that is to some extent incorporated within the Zande tradition. That fuller vision is, of course, present in the Christian tradition within Western culture, but it is not now a central aspect of our way of looking at law.

In this brief analysis of an aspect of Zande culture I have been trying to show that at the origin of language games, paradigms, or horizons that both unite and divide us is the set of fundamental operations by which we are experiencing, intelligent, rational, and responsible subjects. These fundamental operations are not propositions, although if the operations are understood, the understanding will be expressed in propositions and sentences.

I have compared Zande practice with our court procedure. The basic points of comparison were the operations of asking certain kinds of questions and giving certain kinds of answers. Whether or not the Azande raise questions and seek true answers is a thoroughly empirical question. All the evidence available to me is that they do, and I have no grounds for thinking that they do not, but this should not conceal the fact that the question is empirical. Again, whether or not the readers of this study ask questions and seek true answers is, for me, an empirical question. Once more, I have no grounds for thinking that they do not.

What are my grounds for thinking that someone I am dealing with raises questions and seeks true answers? In the end, the evidence is provided in the practice of conversation. I know that my conversational partner raises questions and seeks true answers by understanding that person's actions, which I observe as I might observe the activities of a cat. I know a cat does not raise questions and seek true answers simply because the data that I have on the cat's behavior are insufficient to ground that judgment and sufficient to ground the judgment that it does not. My own cognitional operations are present to me as I perform them; I am present to myself in my own cognitional operations. I come to know these operations by turning my attention to them, by working out a theory, and by judging that theory to be correct. The method in both cases is empirical but the data are different.

If my conversational partner utters the sentence, "I wonder whether a circle is a type of ellipse?" I usually take this to be sufficient evidence that he is asking a question. I might, of course, be wrong. I might have simply overheard the sentence and taken it that someone was asking the question, only to discover that the voice was from a tape recorder. Or the person, whom I both saw and heard uttering the sentence, might turn out to have been doing no more than reading a text illustrating a syntactical point in English. The point is not that my judgments are infallible; it is simply that my judgments are based on the evidence I have and on my grasp of its sufficiency. Finally, the world might have been such that I was the only person ever to have raised a question and looked for a true answer. But there is no evidence that this is the way the world actually is and fairly abundant evidence for the opposite position.

What, then, of principles and precepts? The ethical principle is the ethical subject. The ethical subject is a sequence of operations. One of the operations in the sequence is a question of the form, What should I do now? It is by raising this question that the person passes from being, potentially or habitually, an ethical subject, to being actually an ethical subject. If one never raises this question, then one is never an ethical subject. If no one ever raises this question, then there are no ethical subjects and no ethical issues whatsoever. But there are no grounds for thinking that this question is never raised and abundant evidence for thinking that it is. Readers can ask themselves whether or not they raise the question, and only readers who do ask ethical questions have any personal internal evidence of ethical action. The only way to persuade someone who denies asking ethical questions is to lead him to notice the ethical questions that he, unnoticed by himself, does in fact ask.

I do not ask what I should do unless I consider the future undetermined in some respect, unless I consider myself responsible in some measure for it. Aristotle, as has been remarked already, wrote that we do not deliberate about those things that (we think) cannot be otherwise. He could have claimed more: not only do we not; we cannot.

If I genuinely ask what I should do, then I must ask it within a situation. The good is concrete and I ask what I should do here and now. But I ask in the situation as I understand it to be. I want to act in the world as it is, but I can deliberate only in the world as I understand it to be. My simple ethical question involves me in the effort to understand the situation. But if one wants to understand something, one begins by paying attention to the data. There emerges, then, from the practice of asking what I should do the precept that I should pay attention to the situation.

In the history of European jurisprudence there have emerged various rules that are sometimes referred to as rules of natural justice. One of these is the injunction to hear both sides in a dispute: *aude et alteram partem.* This is no more than the specialization, for the adjudicative situation, of the general precept to pay attention to the relevant data, and this precept emerges from the spontaneous intelligent and responsible practice of asking what I should do. One does not pay attention to the situation because of the precept; it is not as if the question were open until the precept was promulgated. The precept to pay attention to the relevant data is the expression of the discovery of what one is already involved in.

Once the discovery is made, either in general or in the more specialized context of adjudication, and expressed either in the general injunction to pay attention to the relevant data or in the more specialized adjudicative rule to hear both sides, then the expressed rule may be followed even by those who have no idea where it comes from. The adjudicative rule to hear both sides is sometimes written of as a rule of natural justice and sometimes understood as innate. When the rule forms an express part of an adjudicative culture, then it may, and often will, be permissible to appeal against a decision on the grounds that the rule was broken.

I have repeatedly written that there are no innate rules, but I have also claimed that the rule to pay attention to the data and the specialized version of it in adjudication are the expressions of the discovery of a spontaneous (or natural) practice. Precisely what is being asserted and what denied must be made clear.

I am making the following assertions:

The process of asking questions is spontaneous and natural in normal human adults. Human infants are potential questioners and become actual questioners as they are educated within their culture.

The process of asking questions is a conscious activity, but neither necessarily nor normally is it itself the focus of attention. If someone asks whether a circle is a kind of ellipse, attention is focused on circles, ellipses, and their interrelations and not at all on the activity of questioning.

When people ask questions, they are present to themselves as ignorant and in search of answers.

In every natural language there exists some way of distinguishing between questions and statements.

In many natural languages there is not only a way of distinguishing between question and answer or statement but also a set of grammatical nouns such as "question" and "answer" and "statement" and verbs such as "ask" or "answer" by which speakers refer to questions and answers. In many, perhaps all, natural languages, therefore, the following exchange is possible:

A: What is the name of that hill?

B: What did you say?

A: I asked what the name of that hill was.

In those languages where such an exchange is possible, it seems that there is some generally available grasp of the distinction between question and answer that is not simply the conscious practice but the beginning of reflection upon the practice.

I know of no natural language that is wholly devoid of such cognitional-grammatical terms. A preliminary analysis, which has very ordinary practical purposes in mind, seems to be expressed in every human natural language.

The process of asking questions can become the focus or object of attention. One may go beyond simply noticing that one asks questions to ask what a question is, what is involved in questioning, and so forth.

One may propose an answer to the question about the question. This answer will be a theory of the question. As with any theory, it may be correct or incorrect. The assertions made here are elements in a theory of the question and, as such, may be correct or incorrect. For example, the first assertion—that questioning is a spontaneous and natural activity—is not itself the process but a theory, or an element in a theory, about the process.

Part of the process of questioning is paying attention to the relevant data. If this assertion is true, then the assertion is part of a theory of questioning, but paying attention to the relevant data is part of the process since the assertion "Paying attention to the relevant data is part of the spontaneous and natural process of questioning" is true if and only if it is the case that paying attention to the relevant data is part of the spontaneous and natural process of questioning.

The precept to pay attention emerges from an understanding of the spontaneous and natural process. Only in this sense is the precept a natural precept. In other words, there is no innate formulation "Pay attention," but we naturally ask questions and asking questions involves paying attention: to ask a question is to pay attention to data in a particular way. One can look

at a circle and at an ellipse without asking any questions
at all, but if one asks whether a circle is a kind of ellipse
then one looks at them in quite a different way. They
become puzzling. Our questions turn the world into a
puzzle and determine for us which data are relevant and
which not. In themselves data are neither relevant nor
irrelevant; data are relevant only with respect to
questions.

The more specialized adjudicative precept to hear both
sides of the case emerges from an understanding of the
kind of question that an adjudicative question is and
the kind of data that are relevant to it. One is involved
with the question and with the data before one invents
the formal rule to clarify the practice.

In summary, then, the formulated rule is in no sense
given, in no sense innate. The practice is given. The
rule formulates and expresses an understanding of the
practice. If and only if the understanding is correct and
the formulation adequate does the rule illumine the
practice.

When we ask a question we spontaneously attend to
data, but there may be interference with our practice.
We may be biased; that is, we may prefer one solution
to another and so overlook data that might exclude the
preferred solution. We may be lazy or tired. We may be
impatient. The list of possible types of interference is
long, but the possibility of distorting interference reveals
that we are responsible for our questioning practice. The
rule catches and stresses this responsibility.

There is no suggestion here that the precept to pay
attention is the only one associated with the practice
of questioning nor that every precept or rule whatsoever
is related to practice in this way. To clarify this point
it is worth looking briefly at two other rules.

A second adjudicative rule, sometimes called a rule
of natural justice, is that no one is to be a judge in his
own case: *nemo iudex in causa sui.* This rule operates

quite explicitly in many legal systems, and if it is
breached one may claim to have the decision set aside
on that account alone. Within the legal system as operating there is usually nothing to be gained by asking
for the source or ground of the rule; it is enough that
the rule exists and that one may rely on it. For our
quite different purposes, however, that question is
pertinent.

Once again, there is no sense whatsoever in which
the rule is given or innate.

It is we, not abstract beings, who ask questions.
Questioners are actual human beings with their histo-
ries, their desires, their backgrounds, their self-interests,
and so on and on. Bias exists. It can in principle be
overcome, but to overcome it is difficult and more
difficult still when one's own interests are involved. *Quod
enim mavult homo verum esse, id potius credit*: for what
one would like to be true, that one more readily believes.

In our legal system the judge and jury are not simply
theoreticians. Their judgments and decisions are not
simply fallible, even if carefully grounded, propositions,
as are, in principle, the propositions of scientists. The
judgments and decisions of judges and juries are taken
as true (*res judicata per verum tenetur*) and are acted
upon; they constitute the human world. Judges and
juries are in a powerful social position to ensure that
their own interests are realized. Since a central issue in
an adjudicative system is the unbiased distribution of
entitlements, it is reasonable to establish a procedure
from which a very obvious and pervasive source of bias
is eliminated.

Since it is in principle possible to overcome bias, in
principle possible to decide against one's own interest
(in the narrow sense), it is in principle possible to be
an unbiased judge in one's own case. But the temptation
remains and over time and different judges and juries

it seems unlikely that the temptation would always be resisted successfully. The rule acknowledges this.

The source of the rule of natural justice that no one should be a judge in his own case is, then, quite banal and totally unmysterious: it is no more or less than an effort to remove a systematic and regular source of bias. Its source is twofold: on the one hand, the discovery that the point of an adjudicative system is to decide without bias; on the other hand, the discovery that bias is a constant temptation when one's own interest is involved.

The two rules I have examined are related to the procedure of adjudication itself. In my third and final example I want to look at a set of rules governing a social practice. The social practice is that of lending and borrowing; the set of rules is the set in the French *Code Civil* (Titre Dixieme Articles 1874–1914).

The *Code* begins with a definition of the practice. Lending and borrowing are distinguished from giving and taking. Here the *Code* does no more than state what the practice is and what everyone in the community knows that the practice is. Even children distinguish between giving something "for a loan" and giving it "for keeps." It is quite possible to imagine a society in which lending and borrowing simply did not occur; in such a society there would be no laws governing lending and borrowing.

The *Code* then distinguishes between a loan for use and a loan for consumption. This distinction is used by Aristotle as a commonplace, is expressed in Roman law, and the immediate literary sources of the *Code* are, of course, earlier formulations. But the distinction expresses an understanding of the social practice where two kinds of thing are lent and borrowed. A book is lent so that it may be read, a kind of use; sugar is lent that it may be consumed. (One may complain that consumption is a kind of use, which is true, but this is the kind of verbal complaint that the wise do not indulge in: *de verbis non curant sapientes*.) The distinction between a loan for use and a loan for consumption may not be so explicitly made in common speech, but everyone who lends a book expects to get the same book back and everyone who lends sugar expects to get back the same amount of sugar—but not the same grains. The distinction in the *Code* expresses an understanding of the practice.

The *Code* then asks about ownership. If *NN* lends a book to *AA*, who now owns the book? The answer in the *Code* is that *NN* still owns the book. If *NN* lends sugar to *AA*, who now owns the sugar? The answer in the *Code* is that *AA* now owns the sugar.

At this point the *Code* goes, I think, beyond the everyday. It raises questions that are rarely raised in daily life. Nonetheless the questions are intelligible and the suggested answers hardly unacceptable when one thinks about them. I suspect every reader would accept the *Code*'s answer about the book: the lender remains the owner.

The second answer is, I have discovered, less immediately acceptable, but, on reflection, most people find it at least plausible. If the lender still owns the sugar, once the borrower has consumed it, the borrower remains eternally in the lender's debt, which is implausible. But if the lender no longer owns the sugar, what does he own? The answer is that he owns the right to be given back an equivalent amount of sugar. The borrower owns not only the sugar but the debt.

The brief discussion of the second question throws light back onto the first answer. The lender owns not only the book that he has lent but also the right to be given back the same book; the borrower owns the debt to give back the book.

Further questions arise. When the lender has lent the book is he entitled to take it back at once? The *Code* suggests that the borrower is entitled to keep the book until it has been read. The lender, then, although he still owns the book, has given up his entitlement to its use for the time being. The borrower, therefore, owns not only the debt to return the book but also the entitlement to use it.

Still further questions arise about how long the borrower is entitled to keep the book, how long may elapse between borrowing sugar and returning the equivalent, whether one may use a borrowed book as one might use one's own, and so on. Further detailed analysis of the French *Code Civil* is not germane to our present purposes. It is, however, important to notice what the *Code* does and, equally importantly, what it does not do. It does not impose a set of arbitrary rules on top of a social practice. Rather it is an attempt to understand a social practice from the point of view of justice, that is, from the point of view of the just distribution of entitlements. The guiding question in this section of the *Code* is simply this: Who owns what in the social practice of lending and borrowing? The answers given in the *Code* are attempts to clarify recurrent disputatious situations. They are not infallible but are subject to dispute, correction, or refinement. Meanwhile, they have a special social place and form part of those judicial things that have been settled for the moment and are treated as true; they are part of the res judicata. They form the social context or tradition.

The social practice of lending and borrowing is a commonplace distribution of goods and entitlements and is part of the larger and more complex social practice of just distribution in general. Just or fair distribution has itself two aspects. There is the very general aspect that states, not what is just but that the just is to be achieved. A situation is just when everyone has what is due. Even without knowing what is due it is possible to desire this situation. However, it is not possible to bring about the situation, except by accident, unless one knows what is due, and so the second aspect of the just is the determination of what is due to each. It is possible to desire the just without knowing what is just. There are, however, some presuppositions. The just situation is achieved when each has what is due. The presupposition is that people have entitlements, that things are due to them, that they own things. What they own, what their entitlements are, what is due to them, remains to be settled, but the possibility of just distribution rests on the fact of ownership or entitlement. If, quite radically, no one owns anything, no one is entitled to anything, nothing is due to anyone, then the question of what is just simply does not arise.

There are, of course, different conceptions of ownership, but there exists no human society from which the practice of ownership and entitlement is radically absent. In Europe in the eighteenth century, a conception of ownership developed according to which the owner of a thing was entitled to deal with it in any way whatsoever; this conception is found in the French *Code Civil*, in the *Constitution of Ireland*, and in a great deal of subsequent political thinking. It is this conception of ownership that was attacked by Proudhon and Marx. It is quite true that ownership in this sense is not found in many societies. But ownership and differentiated entitlement are found everywhere.

From the point of view of justice, a society is a network of entitlements. The discussion of lending and borrowing in the *Code Civil* is a clarification of a small area of that network. In that discussion it is entirely presupposed that the lender owns the thing that he is willing to lend. There may well be further questions about the entire distribution of goods, but lending and borrowing occur within a situation where those larger questions are, for the moment, dormant. Thus, to take another but equally commonplace example, there are very real and important questions about the distribution of wealth in modern Western societies, but the vast business of the buying and selling of real estate is carried on within a social context where those questions are dormant. There are, I think, very real questions about the justice of my salary in the context of other members of the society, but these questions would not be germane to a dispute between me and my employer who had failed to pay me. In many societies, including modern Western society, wealth is importantly distributed through inheritance with a consequent very uneven distribution. But courts deal with disputes over inheritance only within the context of the assumption that inheritance is just. There is, so to speak, a contextual justice, and it is with this that courts for the most part deal.

There is also the possibility of attending, more or less clearly and more or less radically, to the surrounding context. Modern governments attend to this context, to some extent at least, when they redistribute taxation, when they apply tax revenue to this rather than that project. Opposing political positions differ on how wealth is to be distributed.

These are questions of justice. There are different opinions and different options, but beneath the differences is the common agreement that entitlement is an issue. Hobbes was quite correct when he saw that, where everyone was entitled to everything, nobody was entitled to anything and there was no justice.

A tradition of justice is a network of traditional entitlements, an organization of the relations of ownership in a society. And just as we realize our linguisticality in a particular natural language, so we discover entitlement and justice in our particular tradition. The tradition is not infallible, it is not unchangeable, it is not something within which we are radically confined, but it is where we start from. Our tradition is our present society and our present selves, and it is these and nothing else that stand in need of reformation. For nothing else yet exists. Our tradition is to a large extent given us, but fundamentally a tradition is the product of choice. It is the product of many choices, through many years, and what has once been the product of choice will be developed by choice. The tradition brings us to the present moment. The next moment is chosen, only to become itself the tradition from which the next choice must begin. The tradition is the dialectical product of intelligence, generosity, humility, and love and stupidity, greed, vanity, and hate. Since this is so, our attitude to our tradition, to be intelligent, must be dialectically critical.

Fundamentally everything is questionable but not everything is in fact questioned. One does not raise questions about answers with which one is satisfied, for to be satisfied with an answer means to have no further questions about it. This does not mean that there are no further questions, that one will never oneself have further questions, but simply that one does not have questions now. So we accept much of whatever tradition we happen to be born into simply because we have no questions, because that is where we happen to be, and because we need images, questions, or reasons to move us from where we are. Even so, it is never our tradition that is basic but our questioning selves; it is not where we are that is basic but where we may be; our final commitment is not to receiving traditional answers but to asking questions and seeking true answers. For this reason, in an older tradition, conscience, not law, is paramount.

We cannot choose whether or not to be actors. We cannot choose whether or not to be the kind of beings that are in part responsible for themselves and their world. If, as I have argued, the basic criterion is the responsible subject, then our basic responsibility is not simply to realize in practice innate rules but to choose the rules. In the end our responsibility is to ourselves rather than to our tradition. If this is not what the primacy of conscience over law means, then it seems to me to have no practical meaning.

Our responsibility is to choose the good, but to do so we have the prior responsibility to determine what we shall count as good. We live within a tradition that suggests what is good. We become normal adults in a community by accepting in large measure those suggestions. We are our tradition, and to question it is to question ourselves. However, our actual moral lives are by no means the simple application of a tradition. Our actual moral lives are the attempt to discover, in often very complex circumstances, what the good is for us. The discovery of the good is our autobiography.

6. Sources of value

To choose to realize a possibility is to determine that possibility as the good to be realized. Choice orders what is incompletely ordered, specifies what is incompletely specified, determines what is incompletely determined, realizes value. We can ask, then, what are the sources of value.

There are material and formal sources of value. The material sources are whatever is to be ordered; the formal sources are the imaginative and intelligent invention of possible orders, the scrutiny of those possibilities, the reasonable and responsible reflection on those possibilities and suggested values, and the decisions that realize those possibilities. We commonly acknowledge these formal sources in our attempts to give reasons for what we do.

Consider the following conversation:

A: Why did you do that?
B: Because I felt like it.

This very ordinary exchange reveals some important characteristics:

–B understands that A is looking for a reason for B's action.
–B acknowledges responsibility for the action.
–B informs A that the action seemed desirable.
–B accepts desirability as a sufficient reason.

It is important to distinguish between feeling like doing something and accepting that feeling as a reason. It is perfectly possible, and even commonplace, to feel like doing something without accepting that the feeling is a sufficient reason for doing it; it is equally possible to choose to do something one does not spontaneously feel like doing. So, in itself, to feel like doing something is neither a sufficient nor a necessary reason.

The imaginary conversation could be continued:

A: Why is "feeling like doing it" a reason?

How is B to answer this second question? It is to this that I now turn.

When we are asked why we have done or chosen something we acknowledge at once the propriety of the question; we accept that we must account for our responsibility. What is sometimes overlooked is that we choose not only the action but also the reason for the action. If I am asked why I chose to write this monograph and if I acknowledge that the question is a proper one, then I must accept responsibility both for writing the monograph and for the reason I give for having written it. Consider the following, not necessarily incompatible, reasons that I might give:

Because I felt like it
Because I thought it would make money
Because I thought I had something to say
Because I thought it would bring me fame of a sort
Because someone suggested that I do so

Putting aside for the moment how adequate the questioner might consider any of these reasons, the crucial fact is that if I give one of them seriously as a reason for my action, then I am taking responsibility for the reason as well as for the action. I am taking responsibility for the action informed by the reason.

In the case of each of the suggested reasons there is a fact that is simply a fact. The fact becomes a reason only because I choose to make it a reason. This may be clarified by looking at another kind of reason. Had I answered the question by saying

Because I am neurotically compelled to write

I would have given, as a reason, a fact from which the writing of the monograph emanated without choice, a fact, therefore, that I did not choose as a reason.[46]

Further clarification may be had by considering what every reader will consider a foolish answer. What kind of reason should I have given had I answered

Because oranges are fruit?

One may be tempted to say that this is simply not a reason at all; that it purports to be a reason of the first kind—like, for example, "Because I felt like it"—but that it fails to be a reason. Now I fully agree that no reader is likely to accept it as an adequate reason, but what the reader will or will not accept is not the point. The point is whether or not I can choose it as a reason.

I have been suggesting that reasons are not simply given but are chosen. I may, for instance, choose the desire for fame as the reason for writing. The desire for fame, I suggest, is present before it becomes, by choice, a reason. I am now asking whether any fact at all can become a reason and have, quite deliberately, chosen what I expect every reader will consider a totally irrelevant fact.

Let us be clear that the fact that oranges are fruit can become a reason for certain actions without any difficulty or oddity: for example, if one were asked why one had displayed the oranges beside the apples and the bananas one might well reply, "Because oranges are fruit."

The oddity, therefore, is not that oranges' being fruit can never be a reason for action but that their being fruit does not seem to be a reason for writing a book.

If someone seriously proposed this as a reason for writing a book either one would dismiss him out of hand or one would go on to ask how and why that was a reason. Eventually, if an answer were to be satisfactory,

a context within which the proferred reason were ac-
ceptably a reason would have to be developed. We are
disinclined to accept the fruitiness of oranges as a reason
for writing a book because we find it difficult to imagine
a context within which it would be a reason. Notice
that we do not have to share the context, merely to
imagine it; it is very easy to understand that a fact or
supposed fact would be a reason for another but not
for oneself.

If this analysis is correct, then the answer to the
original question becomes plain. I cannot choose the
fact that oranges are fruit as a reason for writing a book
unless I operate in a context within which it is an
intelligible reason for that action. But what is true of
this absurd example is true of manifestly acceptable
examples also. Thus, a desire for fame is a possible
reason for writing only in a context within which a
desire for fame is intelligible as a reason.

I have suggested that a desire for fame is not given
as a reason. I have suggested that, if it becomes a reason,
it is chosen as one. Before that choice, it is simply a
fact but yet not a neutral fact. More generally, desire is
not automatically a reason for action, but neither does
it stand neutrally with respect to action.

Desire orients toward fulfillment of a certain kind.
Choice is the ordering of what is incompletely ordered,
but what is incompletely ordered is not a neutral mass
of possibilities but a network of desires, of orientations.
To understand why and how desire for fame may be a
reason for writing one must understand two things:

1. One must grasp the relation—which is obviously
   social—between writing a book and achieving
   fame.
2. One must appreciate the desire for fame.

The first of these is clear and commonplace. The second
is crucial. One finds oneself grasped by the desire,

oriented by it; the desire suggests and orients. By choosing to realize that orientation, one chooses that desire and that orientation as a reason or ordering principle.

The desire is given and, as given, is so far unquestionable. But the desire as chosen is not unquestionable for the choice pretends to be reasonable and so fundamentally open to question.

To claim that the desire for fame is given is by no means to claim that it is innate or that no investigation as to its source is possible. Nor is it claimed that the desire for fame is universally present. The claim is crucially different from any attempt, however oblique, to find a reasonable source for action in prereasonable desire.

Desire for fame is simply an example of a desire that the ethical actor may discover in himself and that reveals him to himself as, at that moment, oriented in a certain way toward his own future. As he takes responsibility for his future, the actor may ask whether or not that orientation is to be realized, whether or not it is an adequate principle to guide his choices, whether or not he will henceforth—for the sole ethical question is what he will henceforth do and become—live his life following the lineaments of that desire. The desire is, at that moment, given; it is part of the material to be organized.

How that moment has been reached is a historical question that may be relevant in the effort to come to a responsible decision. It may well be that earlier choices have contributed greatly to the present givenness of the desire; it may well be that obscured responses, the stuff of a historical psychoanalytic investigation, have largely contributed to its present force; it may well be that this desire is enshrined, more or less clearly, more or less ambiguously, in the culture. These are important aspects of the present that the ethical actor may need to consider. Nonetheless, the fact remains that the desire is now given. The desire is present in the particular ethical actor with some particular intensity. It is present within a complex of other desires, of other needs, of real possibilities, of remembered successes and failures. That orienting complex is where the ethical actor now is.

To choose the desire for fame as a reason for writing a monograph is, in our culture, intelligible both to the one who chooses it and to his companions. It is worth distinguishing between the initial intelligibility of a reason and its eventual complete reasonableness.

That "because oranges are fruit" is, within our culture, unintelligible as a reason for writing a monograph has probably met with little resistance from readers. But an important point may have been missed precisely because the unintelligibility is so patent. The significant and important point is that the actor must choose as a reason for action something that is intelligible to him. I simply cannot choose "because oranges are fruit" as a reason for writing a monograph because it is unintelligible to me as a reason.

Suppose that instead of giving what for most readers is a manifestly unintelligible reason for writing a monograph, I gave the reason, Because I want to save my eternal soul. What would be the status of that suggested reason in our civilization? This is properly a sociological question. Given appropriate interpretive transformations of the phrase "save my eternal soul," that reason is, as a matter of fact, perfectly intelligible to me. Perhaps most readers will sufficiently share the historical sources of Western culture to find it intelligible. They may not accept it as a reason but they will find it intelligible as a reason. But if they do not accept it as a reason, this is because they do not accept the worldview within which it is a reason. If they find it intelligible, this is because they understand the worldview.

In other words, not anything at all but only what is intelligible can be chosen as a reason. This is not surprising since the fundamental character of our re-

sponsibility is that we want to make our lives reasonable
and intelligibility is a necessary, but not a sufficient,
condition of reasonableness.

I can, therefore, choose the desire for fame as the
reason for writing a monograph. Now the next question
arises: Is that choice reasonable? It is this further question that organizes Plato's dialogues. Callicles' reasons
for action are perfectly intelligible to Socrates, but they
do not seem to him reasonable and it is their unrea-
sonableness that he tries to unveil. Socrates' reasons are
scarcely intelligible to Callicles, and it is their intelligibility that must be revealed before their reasonableness
can be shown.

If I now claim that the desire for fame is my reason
for writing this monograph can my interlocutor make
any reply beyond simply accepting this?

The first and most obvious riposte should be disposed
of at once. My interlocutor may point out that writing
the monograph will not result in fame for me and that
I am sadly mistaken. This riposte comes from within
my own worldview or context. My companion, who
shares my view and accepts the desire for fame as a
principle of action, simply tries to convince me that this
particular act will not achieve its stated goal. We can
leave this commonplace aside.

My companion may be one who considers that the
desire for fame is not a satisfactory principle of action.
He understands my context and so finds my reason
intelligible but does not share it. His only recourse is
to do what Plato did: raise questions in an attempt to
undermine my context.[47]

Of course, not just any questions will do. He will get
nowhere by asking me what is the square root of minus
one. The undermining of a context is a subtle operation
requiring an exceedingly flexible intelligence. Plato knew
this. Plato possessed such an intelligence. He knew that
it was a rhetorical activity and knew that truth could

easily lose itself in the thickets of discourse. But this is what Plato's dialogues are about and this is their lasting importance. The idea of distinct intellectual contexts or worldviews or perspectives or presuppositions is crucial to contemporary philosophy, but, although differently, it is crucial to Plato for unless one supposes that Plato was quite clear about people's being in different worlds, his dialogues become meaningless. At the close of the *Gorgias* Socrates tells Callicles that their loves are different and lead them in different directions toward different and opposed values. The different loves are different worldviews, contexts, and so on.

The question as to how my companion might undermine my choice of fame as a reason is not a general question but begins a task specific to me, for it is I who is to be undermined. I do not suppose that I am in every way different from everyone else, but neither do I suppose that I am exactly the same. My companion might ask whether I were prepared to do anything whatsoever to achieve fame or whether I would be prepared to do only certain things. As a matter of fact, I should have to answer that I should be prepared to do only certain things, that I should be prepared to do X but not Y, and so on. My companion might bring me through my imagination to discover more exactly just what I should be prepared to do and what not. And this process would reveal to me that sheer fame was not for me an adequate principle.

To continue the analysis would be tedious. Enough has been said to reveal the method. The reference to Plato is enough to suggest that it was his method. And if the immediately preceding paragraph is examined, it will be seen to be a truncated and condensed Platonic dialogue.

But when we do ask why someone does something, performs a particular action, then the action has been already suggested or is in train or has been completed.

This question is fundamentally about the reasonableness of an already contemplated or completed action. There is, however, a prior question: What am I to do now? Here I am not asking about the reasonableness of a proposal, for nothing has yet been proposed.

When this latter question is genuinely asked, the answer is not yet present; the range of possibilities from which the eventual answer must emerge may not yet have been invented. Where, then, do these possibilities come from? There are material and formal sources. The material sources are the real possibilities of the situation; the formal sources are the emergence and invention of possibilities in the questioner.

The real possibilities of any situation are, we may suppose, not in any relevant sense infinite but they are many. Among the many real possibilities is a smaller range of possibilities that occur to the particular person on a particular occasion. The emergence of that smaller range is influenced by the desires, interests, knowledge, habits, and so on, of the person.

Indeed, the situation itself is in part defined by these. Many times daily, people ask themselves what is now to be done and this commonplace and often repeated question defines what the situation effectively is. Sometimes—traditionally in Western culture at the beginning of a new year, which thus becomes the often trivialized symbol of profound transformation—people may ask themselves what is to be done with their lives as a whole. And they may ask this question with greater or less scope and attention. Sometimes this question is asked at what seems a crucial turning point in their lives: again the tradition presents certain situations as more crucial than others, for example, certain ages, completion of school or college, loss of a job, and so on. Thus, the relevant ethical situation is produced by the precise character and range of the ethical question; it is not simply the surrounding world; it is the world including oneself illuminated by the extent to which one is, at this moment, putting oneself in question.

The range of possibilities that are thrown up, that one invents is, then, regularly defined by the scope of one's question. Even so the possibilities that do in fact occur, occur not in some abstract situation nor to some abstract person. They occur within a particular person within a particular situation. Because our desires tend to their realization, there will be thrown up for consideration possible courses of action that would realize them. In other words, within the range of possible actions that in fact emerge are those that reveal, to us and to others, our desires. They are, as it were, the transformation of inarticulate or nonarticulated desire into the possibility of value.

When we ask what we are to do, what we are to become, we want to make intelligible and reasonable sense of our selves. We recognize this as our responsibility. We may fail to be responsible, but we cannot avoid the demand to be responsible. We begin from where we happen at that moment to be for there is nowhere else from which we can begin. We have no innate axioms from which we can derive solutions. We try to understand, we make suggestions, we raise questions about our suggestions. We know no "reality" against which to check our solutions. We have only the possibility of questioning. The end of questioning is when all questions are answered. The final and unquestionable good is the answer to all questions and to a brief discussion of that good I now turn.

7. The adequate good

Three ways in which an ultimate horizon and ultimate answer might exist have been distinguished previously. The horizon exists as the operative goal of practical or ethical inquiry. Insofar as an ethical actor is within that horizon, the ultimate horizon actually exists as the horizon of that actor. Plato's Royal Ruler in *Statesman* is the exemplar of such an ethical actor. Finally, the ultimate horizon and answer may exist independently of the human ethical actor for whom it is an unknown but intentional goal. The ultimate horizon may exist in itself.

I do not intend to decide the issue of the independent existence of the ultimate horizon. Nonetheless, it may be best simply to state, with no attempt at proof or justification, what my own answer as a matter of fact is. I hold that this answer does exist and I identify it with what, in the European tradition, is, in English, called "God." This answer is in two parts: first, the ultimate good exists; second, it is to be identified with God. No reasons whatsoever are given here—either overtly or covertly—to justify either part of the answer.

Whatever one's position on the existence of the ultimate good which is the answer to all questions, it is wholly implausible to suggest that it is known already. Accordingly, the ultimate good cannot be a known criterion of human action.

I have consistently argued that there are no unquestionable known criteria of human action other than the operative criteria of intelligibility, reasonableness, and responsibility. We do, of course, have known criteria according to which we act, but these criteria are those that we have accepted responsibly, reasonably, and intelligently or irresponsibly, unreasonably, and stupidly and are, themselves, open to question by us as responsible originators of ourselves.

The choices that we make are fundamentally open to question. Choices are to be abandoned when, under questioning, they are revealed to be unsatisfactory. As we move into this incessant process of question, suggestion, question, suggestion, there emerges the overarching question about the process itself. Does it go on forever or has it an end, a limit upon which the questionable suggestions converge?

This overarching question has two possible answers. First, it has no end other than death. Second, it has an end. But what is it that the first answer denies and the second answer affirms? Simply this: that there is an eventual answer, upon which all partial answers converge as upon a limit, that is the answer to all possible questions.

If one's eventual conclusion is that this ultimate answer does not exist, then one's further theoretical question about human ethical action is how to account for reasonableness and responsibility in a situation in which, in the end, reasonableness and responsibility are ungrounded. In his ethical writings, Sartre saw this clearly and set about the task. For this reason, he wrote that existentialism is the working out of the consequences of atheism (where "atheism" means the absence of an answer to all possible questions).[48]

If, on the other hand, one's eventual conclusion is that this ultimate answer does exist, even if it is unknown, then one's further theoretical question is how to account for reasonableness and responsibility in a situation in which reasonableness and responsibility are ultimately grounded.

I have argued that personal responsibility is the criterion for action. The ultimate answer is not a criterion but it is a goal, and so reasonableness and responsibility are fundamentally transcendent, inasmuch as I do not achieve reasonableness and responsibility simply because I choose.

For Sartre, too, personal responsibility is the criterion, but, since the ultimate answer is taken not to exist, choice is, ultimately, the absurd ground, a ground that is not a ground, of action.

Since I have not made any attempt to show that there is such an ultimate answer, I cannot go on to say that Sartre is incorrect. His analysis is correct for a world within which there is no ultimate answer. I have shown here briefly that, in a world in which there is an ultimate answer, reasonableness and responsibility are transcendent and choice is not ultimate.

There are further consequences from the conclusion that there is an ultimate answer. The ultimate answer is the answer to all questions, but one must ask whether that answer is itself intelligent, reasonable, and responsible or simply a complex proposition. I shall not argue the case adequately here. However, the suggestion that the ultimate answer exists independently of the human ethical actor but is no more than a complex proposition is fraught with difficulties. It is difficult to understand how a proposition could actually exist apart from a mind that understands and propounds it.

I have consistently argued throughout this work that propositions are not ultimate but that they have an intelligent, reasonable, and responsible source that, for the propositions we make, is our selves. I suggest, then, that more ultimate than the ultimate answer conceived as a complex proposition is the ultimate answer conceived as emanating from an intelligent and reasonable and responsible source and that it is this source that is ultimate and the ground of intelligibility, reasonableness, and responsibility.

However, if one assumes that the ultimate is intelligent, reasonable, and responsible, then the question arises of the relations between that intelligence, that reasonableness, and that responsibility and the intelligence, reasonableness, and responsibility that we ourselves are. Clearly, that question is blocked by the prior assertion that there is no ultimate answer or by the assertion that the ultimate answer is simply a proposition.

In the Western tradition that question has been answered by a variety of theories and images of inspiration, influence, and grace. I make no attempt here to expound, much less to defend, these. My purpose is simply to show how a series of questions arise in one context and not in another, just as I showed earlier in the case of the Azande and us.

Theoretically the question as to the existence of an ultimate answer marks a bifurcation. Either the ultimate answer exists or it does not. If it does not, one's own choice is ultimate and the intentional goal of action is, in the end, the sign of the absurdity that Sartre considered it to be. If it does, one's own choice is ultimately grounded in an unknown good.

With respect to that bifurcation there are three possible positions. First, one affirms the existence of the ultimate answer. Second, one denies the existence of the ultimate answer. Third, one is undecided.

I have stated what I hold to be the case, but I have offered no arguments to justify my position. My point was simply to show that the question is crucial for an understanding of human ethical action, for our actions occur in the world and cannot be properly understood unless we understand the world in which they occur.

8. Commitment

What of commitment? We may commit ourselves to our operations, that is, to asking questions and seeking true answers. We are, but differently, committed to our answers. Commitment to our operations is commitment to ourselves as ethical agents; it is enduring. Commitment to answers is provisional for answers are provisional and asymptotic, approaching truth and goodness as to a limit but nonetheless real and necessary. From both commitments we can, in different ways, decline.[49]

There is now a common view that, in basic moral disagreement, there is nothing to appeal to in the other. On the position set down here, what is common to us all is a set of operations and to these we may appeal. It may well be that there are no answers to appeal to or that, in the practice of our actual conversations, we do not discover common answers. It is the fact that we share these fundamental operations, that we are these operations, that makes conversation fundamentally possible, although neither easy nor guaranteed. In Platonic terms we are dialecticians rather than merely rhetoricians. We can break through the confines of the horizons within which we now are. But, as Plato shows dramatically in *Gorgias*, the enlargement of horizons is not automatic and Callicles ends where he began. Our responsibility is to seek; to find is grace.[50]

Callicles ends where he began. I have returned repeatedly to the refrain that we begin from where we happen to be. Where we happen to be is, materially, where our culture placed us, but we are, within our culture, transformers of our culture and ourselves. We are present to ourselves as desire and at any moment we are that desire that has been partially imposed and partially chosen. Our autobiography is the history of the transformations of that imposition and those choices. Nothing that Socrates can say, no arguments that he can muster, no images or symbols that he can display deflect Callicles from his present desire. There is, in one sense, nothing in Callicles to which Socrates can appeal. In another sense, there is something to which Socrates can appeal: namely, the possibility that Callicles can be moved. If that possibility is not present, if Callicles is irrevocably his present desire, if he is totally defined by where he now is, then the *Gorgias* is not about Socrates' failure but about his fundamental stupidity for he will have appeared as one trying the literally and manifestly impossible.

9. Rhetoric

I have left readers with nothing more than their vulnerable traditions and their fallible selves. I have tried to remove all trace of a set of incontrovertible, innate, given postulates or axioms.

Incontrovertible postulates or axioms have been removed before by others but often to leave the reader with the paradoxical comfort of relativism. Relativism, as theory, states that there are several, incompatible, incommensurable, equally good contexts defined, however obscurely, by several sets of incommensurable, equally good sets of presuppositions. But if the ethical actor accepts the theory, then he will accept that he is irrevocably within whichever of the incommensurable contexts he happens to find himself. The ethical actor need ask no questions of his context because such questions are unanswerable and he is wholly defined by the limits within which he finds himself. It is a paradoxical comfort but a comfort nonetheless and does not fundamentally disturb the axiomatic image of modern Western thought.

I have suggested that each of us is, at any moment, within his tradition. That tradition is a context that provides answers, suggests values, and we can act within it. But, because the source of reasonableness is thought of as more fundamental than its products, this tradition is not invulnerable. It is open to further questions. Each of us can ask how our present horizon can be enlarged for each of us knows the pressure of unaddressed questions, each of us experiences the traditional ordering as

128

no more than one among many possibilities, each of us knows desires that look for ordered realization.

If it is our questions that move us from horizon to horizon, then ethical rhetoric may be properly more a rhetoric of questions, feelings, and images than it is now thought to be, but as it once, for Plato, more clearly was.

The claim that there is nothing to appeal to in the torturer must be distinguished. We may accept that the torturer affirms, at this moment, no proposition or set of propositions for which an injunction against torture may be deduced. But the torturer can see and hear and feel; he deals with other people in the common run of daily living; he has a history; he has desires; he is in a tradition; he can ask questions; he can understand; he can judge; he experiences a demand for intelligibility, reasonableness, and responsibility. His present is not invulnerable. And it is to this obscure, complex, only partially coherent, vulnerable present that, in ethical rhetoric, we appeal.

Socrates tries to evoke questions in his partners. He does so, in part, by presenting images that, he hopes, will call forth questions. There is no guarantee of success. But that is all we can do. And so to complete the circle: this is what human traditions have always done—presented images in which the imperfect human good is discerned.

Modern ethical rhetoric is a rhetoric of reasons. Commonly when we would persuade someone of the value of a certain attitude or course of action we take the proposed course of action as the theorem to be proved and offer reasons by way of demonstration until we can conclude. This is not so much mistaken as incomplete.

The rhetoric of reasons is present in Plato's dialogues, but, more obviously, there is the rhetoric of question in which the partner's present position is shaken by raising questions that he cannot answer. Questions disturb but do not conclude. They invite transformation but do not necessarily bring it about.

There is also a rhetoric of image, which is frequently practiced but less often remarked upon. In a passage on how we bring someone to understand a problem St. Thomas writes that the teacher "organizes the image so that the learner may see the solution in it." When a listener fails to grasp our meaning we invent a new expression (organize the aural image) in the hope that understanding will dawn. The learner's understanding cannot be commanded. What is appealed to in the learner is not present knowledge: by definition, the knowledge that is to be communicated is absent. What is appealed to is the present fact that the learner is capable of learning; what is appealed to is a possibility. The hope is that the possibility of understanding will be realized through the image.

What is true of theoretical puzzles holds for ethical discovery. When an unassailable ethical proposition is called for, often something like the following is offered:

It is wrong to inflict gratuitous pain on innocent children.

I do not have to deny that many readers, perhaps every reader, will agree with this proposition. But what if someone does not? How can such a person be persuaded? Only, I suspect, by the rhetorics of question and image. But ethical imagery is not the abstracted imagery suited to theoretical inquiry; ethical imagery is the appeal to the incompletely formulated wealth of feeling and desire, and it is here that the association between art and ethics must be investigated. Imaginative shifts call forth new and different possibilities for critical reflection, but the imaginative shifts are not themselves complete just as the images presented to the student to facilitate learning are not complete knowledge. George Steiner has often asked why it is that literature does not always humanize.

The general answer is here: literature expands or contracts the imagination, but ethical action requires the further moves of the invention of possibilities, critical reflection, and decision.[51]

The rhetorics of question and image are not dominant in philosophic discussion of ethical action, but they are, I think, centrally present, in various guises, in psychotherapy and analysis. For when these approaches eschew "morals" as they often claim to do, what they repudiate is deduction of action from a given set of propositions in favor of a dialectical movement through imagery and interrogation of the present, including the past within the present, to an as yet unspecified goal that is the end of therapy and the name of which, although they do not use the term, is "the good."

Notes

1. Moral action without theory

1. This empirically observable distinction between good and bad actions is an expression in action of what has been called a "first principle" of human action, and that, when understood theoretically, may be expressed in the traditional formula that "the good is to be done." The thesis put forward here is that this formula is not a known rule to be followed but is a theoretical element in some theories of action.

2. The classic text on rites of passage is Arnold van Gennep, *Rites de Passage* (Paris, 1909), but since then the ubiquity of these rites throughout the world has become well known. The rite of passage tells the neophytes what it means to be human and inducts them into that social status. Often, through associated tests, the young adults are educated into the feelings and responses thought appropriate to their new status.

3. Many societies distinguish their members according to *what* they know; what began in fifth century B.C. Greek thought was a distinction between *kinds* of knowing: between "common sense" and "theory." That some such distinction exists has since been a constant topic of Western philosophy; precisely what the distinction is and how it is to be applied are matters of continual dispute. Behind this work is Bernard Lonergan's analysis in *Insight: A Study of Human Understanding* (London, 1957).

4. The story of Leonidas and his companions is a story of bravery in two distinguishable senses. First, it is the history of brave men. The story looks outside itself to the real actions that it describes and to which it refers. Second, the story is told in such a way that the listeners will understand what bravery is. It is a presentation of bravery. Aristotle thought that it fell to philosophy to explain bravery—in this he agrees with Plato—and he undertakes this task in the *Nicomachean Ethics*. But in the *Poetics* (chap. 9) he recognizes that the story or play is also an expression of some

133

understanding of bravery and for that reason more philosophical than history. By "history" he means not narration primarily but the historical action itself, including the myriad irrelevant details that obscure the form of bravery that the play presents and the philosopher elucidates. His teacher, Plato, also thought that the function of the text was to reveal the character of bravery, and for this reason, in *Ion*, his chief complaint against the poets is that they do not know that about which they purport to speak. The difference between Plato and Aristotle is not that Aristotle was content to allow the poets to write from ignorance whereas Plato required knowledge; the difference is that Plato thought the poets were ignorant and Aristotle thought they had some understanding. Exactly the same difference between them appears in their different accounts of the competence of judges in Plato's *Statesman* and Aristotle's *Ethics*, in Plato's account of *epieikeia*, or "equity," and Aristotle's account of both "equity" and prudence. For a discussion of knowledge and poetry see Eva Schaper's *Prelude to Aesthetics* (London, 1968). For Aristotle's treatment of equity see my "Aristotle's Notion of Epieikeia" in *Creativity and Method*, ed. M. Lamb (Milwaukee, 1981). Alaisdair MacIntyre in *Whose Justice? Whose Rationality?* (Notre Dame, Ind., 1988) also notices the importance of prudence in Aristotle's discussion of justice. See also Pierre Aubenque, *La Prudence chez Aristote* (Paris, 1963).

5. On the literary character of the Bible see Northrop Frye, *The Great Code* (London, 1982).

2. The ethical field

6. That the ethical field is to be defined as the domain of deliberation and choice is radical, clear, and theoretically coherent but it is not new. It is to be found in Aristotle's *Nicomachean Ethics* and in Thomas Aquinas's treatment of human action in his *Summa Theologiae*, Ia-IIae, which deals with the human "to the extent that humans are principles of their own operations" (Prologue) and in which, from the First Article of the First Question, a distinction is made between "properly human actions" that "proceed from deliberation and choice" and actions that occur in humans but are said "not to be proper to humans since they do not belong to humans inasmuch as they are human." Examples of these are

"involuntary movements of foot or hand or stroking one's beard," and these are said not to be "proper to the human since they do not proceed from deliberated choice [*ex deliberatione rationis*] which is the principle of human actions." St. Thomas's use of the term *principle* here is worth noting. It is obviously not a proposition but is rather the operational source of action.

The restriction of "morality" to a reduced part of the field is notably present in the contemporary debate on "law and morality" and reduces the theoretical significance of that debate very considerably.

7. The distinction of reasons for action into "moral" and "practical," which seems now very prevalent in Western culture, has a historical source in the writings of William of Occam, for whom "moral" action involved obeying or disobeying God's law, which might well have been other than it is: "Accordingly, sin is nothing other than doing or not doing something because God ordered it towards eternal damnation. And God could well have ordered things otherwise" (In. Sent., IV, questions 8–9C). See Michel Bastit, *La Notion de loi de Saint Thomas à Suarez* (Unpublished doctoral thesis, Rennes, 1986). "Practical" actions, for Occam, seem to be actions that are not ordered by God toward salvation or damnation but are related to the everyday conduct of social and political life. The social and political consequences of this theory have been disastrous.

3. Ethical theory

8. Not only do we find it easy to generalize; we find it impossible not do do so. If someone is offered a fruit new to him but that, after a few bites, he finds that he does not like, he will not easily be persuaded to take what he understands to be another instance of the same kind of fruit. He will have to be persuaded that the first fruit was rotten and that it was "rotten bananas," not simply bananas, that he did not like. Of course, it is true that it is *this* banana and *this other* banana that I do not like, and, of course, it is true that there are real and important theoretical questions about the relation of particular to general—the whole Western tradition is concerned with this issue—but it is equally and importantly true that the spontaneous ability to generalize is not

theoretical nor is it the application of theory; it is, rather, the spontaneous practice about which there is theory, indeed, different and incompatible theories.

9. The phrase "where no law, no injustice" is Hobbes's (*Leviathan*, 1651, chap. 13), but the sentiment is Occam's. The radically significant shift from St. Thomas to Occam is that for the former the principle of action is an operation, or a person who is the subject of the operation, whereas for the latter the principle is a formula.

10. See Hans Kelsen's *What Is Justice?* (Berkeley, 1957) and Chaim Perelman, *Justice, Law, and Argument* (Dordrecht, 1980).

11. There are temptations to be unjust that are related to the virtue of justice, as, for example, when on finding money we are tempted to keep it simply because we should like to have a small windfall. But there are other kinds of temptations, as, for example, when someone finds money and his or her companions jeer at the idea of looking for the owner. In such a situation not only the virtue of justice but also courage is needed. Virtues are developed in action but theoretically discovered in the subsequent analysis of action.

4. The extrinsic norm

12. By "command theory" is meant a theory of ethics within which the command of sovereign to subject is the central element. Hobbes's expression of the basis of the theory remains valuable:

> my designe being not to shew what is Law here, and there; but what is law; as Plato, Aristotle, Cicero, and divers others have done, without taking upon them the profession of the study of Law.
>
> And first it is manifest, that Law in generall, is not Counsell, but Command; nor a Command of any man to any man; but only of him, whose Command is addressed to one formerly obliged to obey him. (*Leviathan* [1651], chap. 26)

That there are commands is hardly deniable and these may be studied. What is questionable is whether the human ethical or moral life is adequately understood on the model of command and obedience.

13. The matter is complicated by the idea that some things are neither bad nor good but indifferent in themselves and bad or

good only by convention. The Sophistic position was that all things were of this kind and Occam's view is a version of this. For the background to Aristotle's discussion of the naturally and conventionally just see Réné Antoine Gauthier and Jean Yves Jolif's commentary *L'Ethique à Nicomaque* (Louvain, 1970). St. Thomas considers that some things are naturally just and some conventionally so in his own commentary on Aristotle *In decem libros Ethicorum Aristotelis ad Nicomachum expositio*, Lectio 12, 1020–1024, where he distinguishes three kinds of the conventionally just: first, when, before the law is made, it does not matter whether this or that be done as, for example, whether a goat or two sheep be offered at a sacrificial feast (the example is Aristotle's); second, when a ruling is adopted for a particular case; third, the decisions of the courts that, of course, regard particular cases. In 1023 and 1024 he considers the relation between the naturally and the conventionally just. In 1023 he suggests that the conventionally just arises from the naturally just as a specification of it (*per modum determinationis*). Thus, he considers that it is naturally just that a thief be punished but a question of convention or further specification to discover what the punishment in the particular case should be. The conventional, for Aquinas, is not arbitrary. The shift from the intellectualist to the voluntarist notion of convention occurs in Occam and remains central ever since. See my "Can the Naturally Just Be Discovered?" in *Contemporary Conceptions of Social Philosophy* (Stuttgart, 1988).

I do not think that St. Thomas considered the proposition "It is naturally just that the thief receive punishment" to be unquestionably known. But, whatever St. Thomas's position, it is important to stress that it is no part of the theory advanced here that such propositions are known in some mysterious and infallible way outside inquiry and argument.

14. It is not at all implausible to take the overarching image of the Bible, and particularly the Old Testament, to be that of sovereign and subject, and it should surprise no one if biblically based ethics retain this image, particularly if the literary character of the sacred writings is overlooked.

15. John Selden, *Table Talk: Being the Discourses of John Selden* (London, 1689; reprinted London, 1906), chap. 78, "Law of Nature." For a good brief discussion of the desire for authority see Chaim

Perelman, *Justice, Law and Argument* (Dordrecht, 1980), esp. chap. 2.

16. *The Dialogue Between a Philosopher and a Student of the Common Laws of England* (London, 1681). This was apparently written in 1666, but Hobbes considered it unfinished and forbade its publication. It was published posthumously.

17. R. G. Collingwood, *An Essay on Metaphysics* (Oxford, 1940). See also his *Autobiography* (London, 1939). Collingwood is neither the first nor the last writer to concentrate on incommensurable worldviews and neither is the idea exclusive to philosophers. In the nineteenth century the idea, present in some fashion since the Sophists, gained prominence in German romanticism, especially in the writings of Herder and Schlegel. It was not simply an arbitrary coincidence that at the same time there emerged the non-Euclidean geometries of Riemann and others. Shortly afterward there arose a new interest in other cultures and the beginnings of cultural and social anthropology. In jurisprudence von Savigny wrote from a similar perspective. Directly from Herder in linguistics comes the Sapir-Whorf hypothesis. The list of historians, literary scholars, historians of science, and philosophers who take the fact of incommensurability for granted is large and crosses several rhetorical boundaries so that Michel Foucault's epistemes are not far from Thomas Kuhn's paradigms.

In his *Philosophy and the Mirror of Nature*, referred to in the text, Richard Roty seems content with pragmatic agreement as a theoretical account of human conversation. I have tried to show that this analysis is insufficiently radical in "Insight and Mirrors," *Method* (Los Angeles, 1986). The history of Western philosophy is, at least in part, a history of the failure to agree, but no philosopher has ever concluded that it is, in principle, impossible to persuade opponents even if the impossibility of doing so in practice, given the limitations of time, energy, or goodwill, is accepted. The fundamental presupposition of the Frankfurt school of Habermas, Apel, and others is that agreement is in principle possible even if, as Alexy has suggested recently, infinite time and infinite goodwill are required for agreement in practice. It seems likely that the apparently innocuous, and commonplace, distinction between "in principle" and "in practice" may need some considerable unpacking.

5. Traditions and operations

18. Radical breaks do occur, but these, like all historical processes, are better understood by historians retrospectively than by contemporaries, who, almost inevitably, and for a variety of reasons, tend to exaggerate the differences between their own time and the immediately preceding one. This tendency to exaggerate is found more or less equally in those who approve as in those who disapprove the changes. The opposing tendency to presume fundamental sameness is also common and is one reason why Thomas Kuhn's *The Structure of Scientific Revolutions* (Chicago, 1960) was thought to advocate irrationalism.

19. Decline as much as development is possible and is equally difficult for contemporaries to discern, even when, as is rarely the case, there is little dispute among contemporaries about the kind of thing that would count as development or decline. Development and decline are judged against a standard, but this standard is not a universal given; it is an invention for which we are responsible.

20. Since not only the content of the ethical classification but the scheme itself is traditional, scholars may confidently expect difficulty in translating the fundamental terms of one classificatory scheme into terms already available in another, and people who go to live in a culture very different from their own will experience that difficulty more existentially. On the other hand, ethical traditions order what is given-as-to-be-ordered in human living and this to-be-ordered-given is in part transcultural, for instance, human offspring take several years before being able to fend for themselves and every culture will deal with this; human offspring need to learn their tradition and every culture will deal with this; every human society is faced with the problem of ordering the fact that offspring are the fruit of sexual union.

21. Deuteronomy 5:16, the version in Exodus 20:12, is only slightly different: Honor thy father and thy mother: that thy days may be long upon the land which Yaweh thy God, gives thee. It is worth mentioning in passing, in the light of note 20, the following passages from the Confucian classic *The Doctrine of the Mean*, chap. 15: "2. It is said in the Book of Poetry, 'Happy union with wife and children is like the music of lutes and harps. Where there is concord among brethren, the harmony is delightful and enduring.

Thus may you regulate your family, and enjoy the pleasure of your wife and children. 3. The master said, 'In such a state of things, parents have entire complacence!'" (James Legge's translation, Oxford 1893; reprinted New York, 1971). The Confucian classics order what is recognizably what Deuteronomy orders. Because the ordering is different the Chinese and biblical family differ; because the material to be ordered is similar the different orderings may be fruitfully compared. See my "Discriminating Classes," *Man: Journal of the Royal Anthropological Institute* 2, no. 3 (1976), pp. 345–355.

22. The classification "honor" survives in modern Western culture in part because the command survives in the tradition even though perhaps now less centrally and because it survives in modern literature, theater, and, perhaps most importantly, popular cinema and television. We know what "honor" is when we know how to use the word, but we know how to use the word because it is still part of our tradition.

23. The Cartesian admonition to start from an unassailable foundation has been very influential. Even if there were the foundational propositions that Descartes sought—I think there are not—the admonition would be mythical and is anyhow not a description of Descartes's own effort. For Descartes did not start from the proposition "I think; therefore I am." He concluded that proposition after a slow and painful inquiry. He began as we all must begin: from where, when we begin, we happen to be. And where we happen to be is where our tradition, whatever it is, has left us. "I think; therefore I am" is not the beginning of an inquiry; it is, rather, the conclusion of an inquiry that began with a question about the foundations of knowing.

24. Since my writing in this neutral way of Coulomb's law, the furor about "cold fusion" arose. The skepticism of some physicists stemmed from their commitment to this law, which the cold fusion experiments seemed to violate. This is simply another clear and contemporary example of our tendency to sift new suggestions through the sieve of our present tradition, and Coulomb's law is a significant part of the tradition of modern physics.

25. In *Whose Justice? Which Rationality?* (Notre Dame, Ind., 1988), p. 11, Alasdair MacIntyre writes of "that unfortunate fiction, the so-called Judeo-Christian tradition." The fictional element is not that Christianity has a Jewish background but the idea that there

is simply a fused tradition that is neither Jewish nor Christian. We may expect that the meaning of honoring parents has developed differently within the two traditions and this is found to be so. Similarly, there is not one single development with the Christian tradition, and the present theory would not expect one.

26. Northrop Frye in *The Great Code* (London, 1982), p. 118: "Whatever the historical facts may have been, the Old Testament's narrative sequence, in which the giving of the law comes so soon after the Exodus, is logically and psychologically the right one. Mount Sinai follows the spoiling of the Egyptians as the night the day. A shared crisis gives a community a sense of involvement with its own laws, customs and institutions, a sense of being a people set apart."

27. It is obvious that an ethical tradition may be used by the powerful to oppress the powerless, and so someone's idea of Christ may be imposed on another, and, in general, what can happen sooner or later will happen. There is no reason to suppose that a noble tradition will be nobly used. Also common is the tendency to present tradition understood in a certain way as "the" tradition, which is then used to define "insiders" and "outsiders."

28. *Leviathan*, chap. 13. In this, probably the best known passage from the book, Hobbes elucidates what Aquinas would call the final cause of human political agreement. The final cause as known (that is, the envisaged result) is the end because of which one acts. Thus, however much Aristotle, Aquinas, and Hobbes are supposed to differ and do in fact differ, it should not be overlooked that insofar as the production of society is a human action in St. Thomas's sense (see note 6) then it is the product of deliberation and choice and on this all three are agreed. They differ in their conception of quite what it is that is produced, and Hobbes's concentration on the sovereign both comes from and leads back into a developing image of the state as total organization. On the image of the state as an order of quite another kind see F. A. Hayek, *The Fatal Conceit* (London 1988). Hayek has an understanding of, and an attitude to, socialism with which I am reluctant to agree, and an enthusiasm for an unfettered market that I do not entirely share, but his idea of an order emergent from many decisions is, I think, fundamental. Hayek's work forces upon us the question, What precisely is chosen in human society?, since, if the social order is the product of many independent choices, then it

would not seem, to be an object of a single choice. The function of government in this conception is to provide a context within which citizens can interact freely, and political choice would have that context as its object. John Gray in his recent *Limited Government: A Positive Agenda* (London, 1989), p. 21, attempts a sharper definition of the meaning of this: "The contours of the sphere of independence are not natural truths, but instead artefacts of law and convention, subject to the need for recurrent redefinition and sometimes expressing a balance between competing interests and values. The ideal of laissez faire is only a mirage, since it distracts us from the task of assessing our historical inheritance of laws and procedures and reforming it so as to promote the diffusion of power and initiative and thus to enhance the liberty and dignity of individuals."

29. Perelman in *Justice, Law and Argument*, p. 28, seems to suggest—though this is not strictly a consequence of his sentence— that philosophers before Hume did not know this: "Since Hume, many have pointed out that one cannot logically deduce a right from a fact, nor what ought to be from what is."

The argument "Adolescent children need their emerging emergent adulthood respected; therefore, we should respect their emerging adulthood" is an enthymeme and, if proposed as a complete argument, is, quite simply, invalid, as Hume saw. The suppressed premise, which would validate the incomplete argument, must contain an "ought." This "ought" is contained, in my colleague John Dowling's formulation, in "the first principle of morality: the power to ask questions of responsibility," which is the source from which the suppressed premise responsibly flows. Still, if the *possibility* of my being obliged has its source in my power to ask questions of responsibility, my being *actually* and *concretely* obliged stems from my actually asking a question of responsibility and responsibly judging that a suggested course of action is required of me.

30. I have suggested that we learn our ethics as we learn our language, but it should be added that we learn our ethics through our language. Thus, we first learn "ought" or "should" by learning how to use and using these words. We weave our lives with a web of learned "oughts" and "shoulds" and, by doing so, learn two things. First, we learn the ethics of our community: tradition. Second, we learn that we are the kind of being that is present to

itself as one that "ought" to do things. There are a number of complexifying features that I shall be content simply to list:

1. The language within which we learn our ethics often includes in some fashion the residue of a theory or theories of ethics and so may at once illuminate and confuse. Thus, an ethical education dominated by the terms "ought" and "should" is almost certainly the residue of an ethics of duty, that is, an ethics within which the dominant image is the obligation to act according to laws.

2. Whatever the tradition encased in the education insofar as it is an ethics, it will refer to and derive its support, however obscurely, from our presence to ourselves as in some measure responsible for our future (although, of course, we do not say to ourselves that we are present to ourselves as in some measure responsible for our future; see section 5.3).

3. Accordingly, in a natural language, we may expect to find signs not only of the fundamental ethical character of its speakers but of every level of ethical theory.

31. Justinian's codification of Roman law, the *Corpus Iuris Civilis*, is systematic inasmuch as it organizes civil law into the law of persons, things, and actions, an organization already present in Gaius' *Institutes*, but it neither is nor pretends to be a consistent set of laws. It is consistent where opinion was settled and, where opinion was not yet settled, it is a collection of noteworthy opinions. See M. Villey, *Le droit Romain* (Paris, 1979). The French *Code Civil*, on the other hand, pretends to be, and largely is, a consistent set of laws and were an inconsistency to be found, an effort would be made to remove it. Still, in jurisprudence, as in other parts of ethics, as in science and common sense, consistency remains a goal: "Existing judgements may be found to conflict, and so they release the dialectical process. Again, though they do not conflict, they may not be completely independent of each other, and so they stimulate the logical effort for organized coherence." Bernard Lonergan, *Insight* (London, 1957), p. 277.

32. It is as well to distinguish between contexts that are genuinely incompatible and contexts that only seem so. In the text is an example of the former. An example of the latter is the commonplace contrast between the following propositions:

The planets move in approximately elliptical orbits with the sun at their focus.

The earth is at rest and the sun rises and sets.

The apparent strain between them becomes real only if one assumes that one is committed to adding to each the restriction "from every viewpoint." If, on the other hand, one adds to the first the restriction "from the viewpoint of explanation" and to the second "from the viewpoint of ordinary description," there is introduced a logical separation of domains that removes the incoherence. As soon as a culture develops distinct domains, the possibility of confusion between them arises; the tendency emerges to allow one domain to dominate to the exclusion of others; spurious questions or presumptions of incoherence arise; a genuine demand for a theory to account for the relations between the distinct domains arises. See Lonergan, *Insight*, chap. 10, section 5.3, pp. 293ff. Ludwig Wittgenstein's proposal that there are distinct language games makes the same point, although some Wittgensteinians seem to think that he meant that genuinely incompatible propositions were true in one language game and false in another, which would make him a radical relativist. Lonergan's account of viewpoints is, to use a metaphor from mechanics, an account of transformations between frameworks. Finally, radical relativism within the one person, who plays several incompatible language games, introduces radical incoherence within the single person or single mind.

33. See his note to chap. 5 of the *Essay on Metaphysics*, p. 48. He does not, however, really come to grips with the strain that this note introduces but retreats from it in chap. 6.

34. One must not invalidly conclude that there are no true or probable propositions of fact or value. The crucial issue is that none is incontrovertible and none is "given" outside the process of inquiry and argument. The consequence is that, since we are responsible for our judgments, we are responsible for the propositions of fact or value that we affirm. That we are inquirers, that we are ethical beings: that much is given. For the rest we are responsible. Sartre's discussions of the nothingness of human consciousness, which sometimes seem very obscure, are efforts to elucidate this. See for a very clear account: Jean Paul Sartre, *Les carnets de la drôle de guerre* (Paris, 1983), Notebook 3, entry for Thursday, 7 December 1939, p. 139.

35. Relativity mechanics is not content to affirm a multiplicity of reference frames. Rather the fact that possible reference frames are infinite raises questions that did not arise within Newtonian mechanics with its assumption of a single reference frame provided by Absolute Space and Absolute Time.

36. For a discussion of "first principles" in Aquinas and Aristotle see Bernard Lonergan's *Verbum: Word and Idea in Aquinas*, ed. David B. Burrell (University of Notre Dame Press, 1967). Since philosophical language is neither technical nor universally agreed, it will be discovered that the term *principle* is often used differently than the way it is used in this section. I have no quarrel with fluid usage, and my analysis does not pretend to be an analysis of usage.

37. The concentration on the relation between thought and language in modern philosophy compels some clarification. There is no suggestion in the text that formal knowledge of the principle of contradiction can be expressed without language; nor is there a claim that language is not an instrument of human knowledge in each of its phases.

38. When faced with what we know to be a contradiction, we repudiate it; that is, the intelligent listener refuses to affirm both "Ireland is an island" and "Ireland is not an island." The intelligent listener requires no formal knowledge of the principle of contradiction, of which he or she may never have heard, and may belong to a culture in which inquiry into human knowing has never arisen. In other words, the intelligent listener will regularly repudiate contradictions—and, in that sense, acts according to rule—but does not follow a known rule in doing so.

39. Some chemists are convinced that aerosol sprays are negligible in their effect on the ozone layer and that emphasis on them distracts attention from the crucially more important effect of the processes of the production of plastic. But if the example is disputed, this serves to highlight the more basic issue that we act within the situation as we understand it to be but exist in the world as it actually is. The possible gap between the imagined world and the real world is one of the sources of learning since, at least sometimes, decisions appropriate to the world as we imagine it to be put the image to the test of experience only to reveal its inadequacy. A trivial but clear example is arriving in time for a train that leaves at noon only to discover that the actual train left at half past

eleven; a less trivial and more tragic example is Shakespeare's *Othello*, the pivot of which play is the difference between Othello's understanding of the world and the way the world really is (which, in the play, the audience knows). Our own position in life is more that of Othello than that of the audience.

40. "Because, as Damascene wrote, human beings are said to be in God's image, inasmuch as by image is meant having intellect, free will and power over self; now that we have considered the examplar, namely God, and those things which proceed from divine power and will, it remains for us to consider his [God's] image, namely the human, according to that aspect of the human in which humans are the principle of their own acts, having free will and power over their own operations." St. Thomas Aquinas in the Prologue to the discussion of human action (*Summa Theologiae*, Ia-IIae). The reference is to John Damascene, *De fide orthodoxa* 1.2 c.12: MG94, 920.

41. An understanding of the ethical principle may be expressed in the traditional formula "The good is to be done." Whether this expresses an adequate understanding, whether it is an illuminating expression of that understanding, in what respects it is adequate and illuminating and in what respects obfuscating: these are further questions. The present work may be read as the expression of an understanding of the ethical principle, a condensed version of which is, The principle of ethical action is that the human subject is present to himself or herself as responsible in some measure for the future. Dowling's illuminating formulation, already quoted in note 29, is that the first principle of morality is the power to ask questions of responsibility.

42. *Philosophy and the Mirror of Nature* (Princeton, 1980). Wittgenstein also remarked that pictures hold us captive.

43. E. E. Evans-Pritchard, *Witchcraft, Oracles and Magic Among the Azande* (Oxford, 1937); Peter Winch, *The Idea of a Social Science* (London, 1956).

44. Donald Davidson, "On the Very Idea of a Conceptual Scheme," *Inquiries into Truth and Interpretation* (Oxford, 1984). At times Davidson seems to suggest that there are not distinct conceptual schemes and that Thomas Kuhn's theory of paradigms or Collingwood's theory of different sets of absolute presuppositions is simply wrong. I think it would be a mistake so to understand Davidson, whose attention is focused on the fact that we can understand "conceptual schemes" other than our own. What Dav-

idson attacks is radical confinement. Michel Foucault claims that thinkers are confined within their given conceptual schemes or epistemes. There is a deep ambiguity here. It is true, but trivially true, that a thinker can think only what he or she can think. It is also true that a thinker can break out of the confines of the surrounding tradition: thus Newton broke out of the system we now know as pre-Newtonian mechanics.

It is also true that we are all limited and that historians of thought can sometimes in retrospect discern limitations and the reasons for those limitations of which the thinker was unaware. Davidson claims that we can understand others from very different worldviews than our own; he does not claim that such understanding is automatic, easy, or infallible.

If two thinkers, A and B, are thinking within distinct worldviews, then A will have at least one thought that B cannot have as long as B remains in a worldview different from A's. If B is radically confined to that worldview, then quite radically, B cannot think what A can think. But if B, quite radically, cannot think what A can think, the grounds for calling both A and B instances of the same kind of thing become at least uncertain. Furthermore, as I mention in another place, the grounds for radical racism become correspondingly more solid, for radical racism is based on the belief that, say, blacks and whites are not the same kind of thing.

45. From every answer further questions arise. Why, for instance, did the Azande invent witchcraft to account for coincidence? Why did the Sumerians and Babylonians invent astrology to account for coincidence? Why did Christians invent various versions of Providence? It is only a very generic answer—although it remains a genuine answer—to say that all three wished to explain the chance or unintelligible event and that the desire to explain what is not understood is what Aristotle called "wonder" and is the first principle of knowing. To discover how the different questions and answers emerged from and fitted into the surrounding culture is the scholar's task.

6. Sources of value

46. Aquinas knew nothing of neuroses as the source of action; nonetheless, his answer to the objection that some activities occur without deliberation is pertinent:

To that objection we may say that such actions are not properly or specifically human as they do not proceed from deliberation and choice which is the proper specific principle of human action. Accordingly, they have, so to speak, an imagined goal, rather than one established reasonably. (*Summa Theologiae*, Ia-IIae q. 1, a. 1, answer to the third objection)

To the extent that the source of the writing is neurotic compulsion, the writing is not a properly or specifically human act or, in the terms of this work, not properly an ethical act. The significance of this for the relation between psychological and ethical counseling is that it clarifies a distinction of domains and indicates why terms and relations appropriate to one are irrelevant to the other and why psychological counseling has as its goal the release of the person into the ethical domain from which the neurosis excludes him.

47. A literary example of the understanding of the desire for fame coupled with a repudiation of its reasonableness is found in the Confucian classic *The Doctrine of the Mean*, chap. 11, 1: The Master said: "To live in obscurity, and yet practise wonders, in order to be mentioned with honour in future ages:—this is what I do not do." And Milton, in *Lycidas*, refers to fame as "the last infirmity of noble mind." But equally within the Western literary tradition is Horace's conviction that his writing was a monument more lasting than bronze, because of which "I shall not wholly die; a great part of me shall live and I shall grow continuously, ever young with the praise of posterity." And Bacon: "Men in great place are thrice servants: servants of the sovereign, servants of fame, and servants of business." And Burke called fame "a passion which is the instinct of all great souls." These indicate nicely the ambiguity inherent in any complex tradition, an ambiguity that is likely to be found in individual members of the tradition. The idea that any one of us is, at any moment in our lives, completely coherent is at once mythical and deeply misleading as a theory of ethics.

7. The adequate good

48. See Jean Paul Sartre, *Existentialism and Humanism* (London, 1973). The differences between my position and Sartre's are rea-

sonably subtle. Sartre rejects God both as the ultimate good and as criterion, but, insofar as he distinguishes between these, which he hardly does, it is upon God as criterion that he concentrates. Human facticity consists in our being simply facts that do not explain themselves and for which there is no explanation; on the basis of this sheer matter of fact we must choose, so that human choice and human value rest ultimately on the merely factual, the unexplained and unexplainable, the ungrounded: "the world of values, necessity and liberty all hang from this primitive and absurd fact" (*Les carnets de la drôle de guerre*, Notebook 3, December 7, 1939). Here Sartre concentrates on the absence of an ultimate ground. But when he discusses God as a possible foundation or ground, he seems to think of God as the provider of basic rules that would, as it were, validate human values: God and rules as criteria. What I have done is distinguish clearly between the ultimate good as unknown goal and given criteria for which we are not responsible, as ultimate arbiters of choice.

8. Commitment

49. Not to choose is not a choice open to us; to have no questions is not open to us; nonetheless, to raise questions responsibly, not to brush aside inconvenient data, to encourage further questions requires commitment.

50. It is a fundamental presupposition of the Platonic dialogues, as it is a fundamental presupposition of real dialogue, that the partners share a deep context. Since Plato is a theorist he attempts to elucidate what that context is and he does so in his theory of *anemnesis*, or remembrance. Fundamentally, humans "know" the real world that they have "forgotten"; the function of discourse is to present images that will "remind" them. The theory of fundamental intellectual operations fulfills here the function that *anemnesis* fulfilled in Plato.

9. Rhetoric

51. George Steiner, *After Babel* (London, 1975). The appeal to an incompletely formulated wealth of feeling and desire may be

misunderstood as a surreptitious attempt to restore shared presuppositions. What is supposed is that present feelings may be appealed
to and altered by symbols and images, whether those symbols or
images be verbal, dramatic, pictorial, kinesthetic, aural, or whatever.
Plato's correlation between musical modes and very specific orientations may be somewhat simplistic, but the basic insight is correct,
important, and, to a large extent, overlooked. It is not supposed
here that the attempt to appeal to feeling, at the level of feeling,
is easy or automatically successful. It is, however, supposed—and
this is the fundamental position on which the argument of this
essay rests—that wherever any human being morally is, at any level
of his or her moral consciousness, at any moment in his or her
life, is never the complete realization of his or her possibilities. In
Sartre's formulation, we are not (actually) what we are (possibly);
in Leibniz's words: our notion is realized only at the end of our
lives; in Aristotelian and Thomist terms, we are always in potency
with respect to the good; in the imagery of the New Testament,
we are not perfect as our Heavenly Father is perfect; in the imagery
of Jeremiah our hearts of stone may be replaced with hearts of
flesh. The answer to Rorty's example of the torturer is that the
person who is the torturer is never simply and irrevocably the
torturer. But contraction is likewise our possibility and "too great
a sacrifice may make a stone of the heart." Corruption, too, is
possible at the symbolic as at any other level. We are fragile and
uncertain beings and an ethical theory must acknowledge this.

Index